IT IS FINISHED

Transforming your life through the finished work of the cross

Nerida Walker

It Is Finished

ISBN 978-981-08-8714-8

www.itisfinishedbook.com

New Life Ministries—Bringing Life To Barrenness
PO Box 593 Forestville NSW 2087, Sydney, Australia.
Email: contact@newlifeministries.com.au
Web: www.newlifeministries.com.au

Published in Partnership

22 Media Pte Ltd
info@22media.co

Harrison House Publishing

Tulsa, OK 74145

Printed in the United States of America
First edition, second print: March 2012

Contents

Acknowledgements

I would like to thank the following people who have been a great source of encouragement and support in my life and ministry.

Thank you first of all to my dear husband, Shaun, for supporting, encouraging and releasing me into ministry. I also thank him for allowing me to spend copious amounts of time on the phone, the Internet and away ministering all around the world. I also want to thank him for helping me to fine tune what I wanted to say and how I put my thoughts together in this book.

Thank you also to our precious miracles, Kaitlin, Aidan, Aaron and Jesse, for being who they are and for sharing me with others by allowing me to pray and minister when needed.

To all my loving friends and family, thank you for supporting me throughout the years with your encouragement and prayers. It has truly helped me to continue to do what God has called me to do.

To the amazing men and women I minister with in **New Life Ministries** and **River Christian Church**. Your time, gifts, talents, skills, love, prayers and support have been invaluable in my life. Thanks for joining me and helping me to continue the work that the Lord had begun. Thanks also for your support and understanding of my absence when away in ministry and also while working on this book.

Thank you also to Debbie Nolan who edited this book. I cannot thank you and your husband, Sean, enough for all your love, support and encouragement.

And, lastly, thank you to the team at 22 Media, for your continued support in helping to spread the truths in God's Word worldwide to help many discover Jesus and how to transform their lives through the finished work of the cross!

About *It Is Finished*

Do you need a breakthrough? Are you tired of being broke, sick, depressed or oppressed? Have you been struggling to see the promises of God come to pass in your life? Well, I have **good news** for you! When you know who you are in Christ and what you have already inherited in Him as a believer, you can see God's power released to transform your life.

Through Jesus we have been given God's power, authority and ability to walk in victory in every area of our lives. But, for many Christians, somewhere along the line, this truth has been lost, such that the things of God's kingdom are foreign to many believers. But this needs to change! We are called to walk by faith and not by sight or appearance, so it is time for the body of Christ to stop asking God to do what He has already done, and rise up and start walking by the truth of who we are in Christ and by what we have **already inherited** in Him.

I have a passion to see believers walk in the fullness of their salvation. My purpose in writing this book is to show you what God has already provided for you as revealed in His Word. I have not left you with knowledge alone, but also with the keys to help you apply this truth so that you can see the fullness of God's provision **become a reality** in your life. While I have specifically covered the most common areas where I find that Christians struggle, these principles can be applied to every other area of life.

It is my heart's desire that you will discover through reading this book that absolutely NOTHING is impossible with God (Luke 1:37, AMP). I pray that you will find this book indispensable in your personal journey and daily walk with the Lord. I encourage you to not just read the truths in this book, but to meditate on them, renew your mind with them and **apply** them to your life. Then, like me, and many others around the world, you can be transformed through the finished work of the cross!

When you do, make sure to write to me and share your testimony!

Nerida Walker

Three Powerful Chapters To Transform Your Life

Three Simple Words... *It Is Finished!*

ONE

When Jesus hung on the cross His very last words before He gave up His spirit were, "It is finished" (John 19:30). Three simple words, yet very powerful in their meaning. Jesus had completed the work He came to do.

Through reading this book, you will discover the fullness of what Jesus purchased through the finished work of the cross. You will learn that He paid the price in full for EVERY CURSE that came into the world as the result of the fall in the Garden of Eden. JESUS REDEEMED US FROM THEM ALL! He bore it ALL on His body; and took it in our place. Jesus is not just our sin substitute, but He is also our substitute for everything that came into the world as a consequence of sin. This means that sickness, disease, poverty, debt, lack, brokenness, depression—you name it, Jesus bore it, disarmed it and conquered it for you!

Before we learn how to apply what was purchased through the cross, it is important first to understand the fullness of what Jesus did and what we have inherited, so that we can live in the fullness of that provision.

What did Jesus do?

- **He became sin**—so you now have complete forgiveness (2 Corinthians 5:21).
- **He disarmed the devil and all his works**—so you now have deliverance and victory over all the power and works of the enemy (Luke 10:19, Colossians 1:13–14; 2:15).
- **He disarmed ALL sicknesses and diseases**—so you now have the provision of healing and you can live in health (Isaiah 53:4–5).
- **He gave you His Word**—so you can discover who you are and what you have **already** inherited (2 Peter 1:3–5).
- **He gave you His power and authority**—so you can now exercise that same power and authority even over your own body, natural symptoms and circumstances (Matthew 28:18–20).
- **He gave you His Spirit**—so you now have His very life, power, nature, character and ability IN YOU through the Holy Spirit who dwells within you (Romans 8:11).

This is just some of what was accomplished! The work of the cross was a complete work. The price has already been paid, the work is already done and the victory already won. For this reason, when it comes to what Jesus has purchased, we don't need to seek, pray, fast or ask for these things because they have already been provided! The Bible tells us that when Jesus ascended into heaven, He sat down! His work was completed! Jesus is now seated at the right hand of the Father—waiting for you to go and possess EVERYTHING that He died to purchase for you! This means that God has already finished His part for us through Jesus. Now, that is good news! Do you realise what that means? If you are in Christ, then you already have your inheritance. And it is through God's Word that we find what has been provided and how to apply it to our daily lives.

> His divine power **has given us** [past tense] **everything we need for life and godliness** through our knowledge of Him who called us by His own glory and goodness. Through these He has given us His very great and **precious promises**, so that **through them** you may participate in the divine nature and escape the corruption in the world caused by evil desires.
>
> —2 PETER 1:3

What more do you need!

God has ALREADY done everything He could possibly do! **IT IS FINISHED**! It is now up to you to KNOW, BELIEVE and ACT on this truth so that you can see His power released to transform your life.

Three Simple Keys...
How To See God's Power Released In Your Life

TWO

When it comes to receiving what Jesus did on the cross, it's not about praying or asking God to do what He has already done! Instead, it is about discovering what has already been provided and then learning how to walk in the fullness of that provision. I believe that there are three simple keys to seeing God's power released in your life to change your natural circumstances:

1) **Knowledge or *Information:*** Knowing what is available to you as outlined in God's Word, knowing the fullness of what Jesus has done and knowing your authority in this world.
2) **Faith or *Revelation:*** Believing that you have received what Jesus purchased through the finished work of the cross by meditating on God's Word until what it says is more real and powerful to you than what your natural circumstances are dictating.

3) **Action or *Application:*** Applying the truth to your life, acting on what you believe and exercising authority over your natural circumstances.

In other words, once you have discovered the truth, take God at His Word and act on what He says! This is how you walk by faith, not by sight, to see God's power released to overcome the challenges you face in every area of your life.

Your Faith In Action

One way we put action to our faith is simply by believing in our heart and confessing with our mouth what God has done through Jesus!

- **Keep God's Word in your heart!**

> My son, **attend to my Words**; consent and submit to my sayings [the NKJV says...incline your ear to My sayings]. Let them not depart from your sight; **keep them** in the centre of your heart. For **they are life to those who find them**, **healing** and **health** to all their flesh. **Keep and guard your heart with all vigilance** and above all that you guard, for out of it flow the springs of life [the NIV says...guard your heart, for it is the wellspring of life].
>
> —Proverbs 4:20–23, AMP

If we want to have the "springs of life" flowing out of our heart, affecting our body, mind and outward circumstances, then we need to keep God's Word before our eyes and ears by reading it, meditating upon it, hearing it preached and hearing our own voice speaking it.

God's Word is alive and full of power (Hebrews 4:12, NKJV). Think about it—when you keep meditating on something that's alive and full of power, it has to bring **healing and health** to your flesh!

In Hebrew, the word "meditate" literally means to immerse your whole self in the truth of what God's Word says by picturing, pondering, imagining, studying and musing it over within your inner man, while also muttering,

uttering and speaking this truth to yourself with the words of your mouth. Joshua was instructed not to let God's Word **depart from his mouth**, but to **meditate on it day and night**, so that he could **observe himself doing** all that it said. This was the key to how he would make his way prosperous and have good success (Joshua 1:8, NKJV). Meditating on the Word therefore is not meant to be a one-off occurrence. Rather, it needs to be continued until revelation comes, and you see your circumstances through the eyes of what it says and not through what you see and experience in the natural realm.

The word "health" in Proverbs 4:22 means cure or remedy. God's Word is the cure or remedy, or the **medicine** that we take to experience healing in our physical bodies! It can also affect and change our outward circumstances for the better. If you went to a medical doctor and he prescribed medication for you to take three times a day, would you take it? Of course you would. You would take it in faith expecting it to cure you. And since God's power is greater than any worldly medicine, it will not only cure the symptoms, but it will also bring healing to what is causing the condition in the first place. Now, that is good news!

- **Keep God's Word in your mouth!**

> ..."The word is near you, **in your mouth and in your heart**" (that is, the word of faith which we preach): that if **you confess with your mouth** the Lord Jesus and **believe in your heart** that God has raised Him from the dead, you will be saved. **For with the heart one believes** unto righteousness, and **with the mouth confession** is made unto salvation."
>
> —Romans 10:8–10, NKJV

The word "confess" in Greek in the scripture above is *homologeo* and means, to agree with, not to refuse or deny, to declare openly, speak out freely. So confession is to agree out of our mouth by saying the same thing as what God's Word says about what He has done for us through His Son!

> The tongue has the power of life and death, and those who love it will eat its fruit.
>
> —Proverbs 18:21

There is power in our words! Our words can either create or destroy. When we speak words of life, we eat the fruit of those life-filled words. Conversely, when we speak words of death, we eat the fruit of those words as well.

- **God's Word is powerful!**

> Through faith we understand that the worlds were framed **by the word of God**, so that things which are seen were not made of things which do appear.
>
> —Hebrews 11:3, KJV

We know from the book of **Genesis** that God spoke and the world was created. God's power was released by His words. When He spoke His Words were full of creative power. They framed and fashioned what He directed.

> For **the word that God speaks** is **alive** and **full of power** [making it active, operative, energising, and effective]; it is sharper than any two-edged sword, penetrating to the dividing line of the breath of life (soul) and [the immortal] spirit, and of joints and marrow [of the deepest parts of our nature], exposing and sifting and analysing and judging the very thoughts and purposes of the heart. [The NIV says… for the word of God is living and active.]
>
> —Hebrews 4:12, AMP

And God has not diminished in power! He is so powerful that the whole universe is still being upheld and suspended in space by His words:

> ...***upholding*** and maintaining and guiding and propelling the universe **by His mighty word of power**…
>
> —Hebrews 1:3, AMP

Jesus was God in the flesh and He was given all of God's power and authority. He in turn gave that same power and authority to all who believe in Him. This means that as God's children, we have the same authority that Jesus has! The Bible says, "as He is, so are we in this world" (1 John 4:17, NKJV)!

When you know who you are in Christ, where you are seated, and understand your power and authority as a believer, you will realise that the way you see God's power released is through your words! God's power penetrates every realm—the physical, spiritual and emotional—and can bring life, health and restoration to your cells, organs and tissues. So if you want to see a change in your natural circumstances, then say what God's Word says about what Jesus has done for you in that area of your life. We don't confess or declare God's Word to get God to do something for us or to make the Word work. We confess what it says because of what God has already done through Jesus' finished work at the cross. This enables you to:

- Declare what Jesus has already purchased for you.
- Declare the truth of what God says about you!
- Transform your natural thinking and understanding until you see your situation through the eyes of faith or through the eyes of what God's Word says.
- Walk by faith (by the finished work of the cross), not by sight or appearance.
- Replace any fears and doubts you have with the truth that sets you free.
- Act on what you believe by taking authority over your natural circumstances.
- Call those things that are not as though they were (Romans 4:17).

> "For assuredly, I say to you, **whoever says** to this mountain, 'Be removed and be cast into the sea,' **and does not doubt in his heart, but believes** that those things **he says** will be done, **he will have whatever he says**. Therefore I say to you, whatever things you ask when you pray, believe that you receive them, and you will have them."
>
> —Mark 11:23–24, NKJV

Stop speaking about the mountains, situations or circumstances in your life and begin to speak to them. Speaking about your circumstances will change nothing, but speaking to them with your God-given authority will.

Therefore...

Let the redeemed of the Lord say so!

As you read through the following chapters, continue to put God's Word in your heart by meditating on the scriptures AND agreeing with what they say by confessing God's Word through declaring the scriptures, prayers and declarations over your life!

God's Kingdom Has Come!

THREE

If we want to see change in our natural circumstances, we need to understand the realm of God's kingdom and how to operate in it so that we can see His kingdom power released in our lives.

> "Do not be afraid, little flock, for your father has been pleased to give you the kingdom."
>
> —Luke 12:32

Many Christians talk about God's kingdom or they hear it being preached, but they never know how to truly experience it for themselves! I believe that there is too much talk about the kingdom and not enough action! There has got to come a time when we stop talking about God's kingdom and start "doing" the kingdom by taking what we know and acting on it, thus entering into all of what God has for us! This is how we will start living and experiencing the kingdom!

God's Kingdom Is Not A Place!

Many misunderstand what the kingdom of God actually is. The kingdom of God is often confused with the kingdom of heaven. It's not difficult to understand why. Both are mentioned in the New Testament. However, they are actually two different kingdoms. The kingdom of heaven is the place where God resides and where Jesus is now seated at the right hand of the Father. However, the kingdom of God is not a physical place at all.

> For the kingdom of God is not a matter of eating and drinking, but of **righteousness**, **peace** and **joy** in the Holy Spirit.
>
> —Romans 14:17

Did you get that? The kingdom of God is righteousness, peace and joy! These three supernatural forces will release God's power into every area of your life! If we can learn to let God's righteousness, peace and joy grow and bear fruit in and through our lives, we will be transformed from the inside out!

There Is Power In God's Kingdom!

God's kingdom is not just His righteousness, peace and joy, but it is also His abundant life, nature, character, ability, rule, reign, dominion, authority and power!

> And my speech and my preaching were not with persuasive words of human wisdom, but in **demonstration of the Spirit** and **of power**, that your faith should not be in the wisdom of men but in **the power of God**.
>
> —1 Corinthians 2:4–5, nkjv

> ...I [Paul] will come to you shortly, if the Lord wills, and I will know, not the word of those who are puffed up, but **the power**. For the kingdom of God is not in word **but in power**.
>
> —1 Corinthians 4:19–20, nkjv

> For our gospel did not come to you **in word** only, but also **in power**, and in the Holy Spirit and in much assurance, as you know what kind of men we were among you for your sake.
>
> —1 Thessalonians 1:5, NKJV

> For I am not ashamed of the **gospel** of Christ, for it is the **power** of God to salvation for everyone who believes…
>
> —Romans 1:16, NKJV

God's Kingdom Is In You!

We have just discovered that God's kingdom is not in heaven somewhere far off. The truth is that His kingdom and everything pertaining to it is within our reach. It is a lot closer and more accessible than most of us realise!

> Asked by the Pharisees when the kingdom of God would come, He replied to them by saying, The kingdom of God does not come with signs to be observed or with visible display, nor will people say, Look! Here [it is]! or, see, [it is] there! For behold, **the kingdom of God is within you** [in your hearts] and among you [surrounding you].
>
> —Luke 17:20–21, AMP

Hallelujah! Did you get that? God's kingdom is IN YOU! But let's keep reading because there is more that I want you to understand.

> But you shall receive power (ability, efficiency, and might) **when the Holy Spirit has come upon you**, and you shall be My witnesses in Jerusalem and all Judea and Samaria and to the ends (the very bounds) of the earth.
>
> —Acts 1:8, AMP

We have already been given the same Spirit of mighty power. The same resurrection power that caused Jesus to rise from the dead is now living and dwelling on the inside of us!

> But if the Spirit of Him who raised Jesus from the dead dwells in you, He who raised Christ from the dead will also give life to your mortal bodies through His Spirit who dwells in you.
>
> —Romans 8:11, nkjv

> ...the eyes of your understanding being enlightened; that you may know what is the hope of His calling, what are the riches of the glory of **His inheritance in the saints**, and what is the **exceeding greatness of His power toward us who believe**, according to the working of His mighty power which He worked in Christ when He raised Him from the dead and seated Him at His right hand in the heavenly places, far above all principality and power and might and dominion, and every name that is named, not only in this age but also in that which is to come...
>
> —Ephesians 1:18–22, nkjv

I encourage you to meditate on these verses until this powerful truth is established in your heart. Remember, it is the truth you KNOW that will set you free!

God's Kingdom Under The Old Covenant

> In this manner, therefore, pray: Our Father in heaven, hallowed be Your name. **Your kingdom come**. Your will be done on earth as it is in heaven.
>
> —Matthew 6:9–10, nkjv

> And He said to them, "Assuredly, I say to you that there are some standing here who will not taste death till they see the **kingdom of God present with power**."
>
> —Mark 9:1, nkjv (Luke 9:27)

In the scriptures above, Jesus was speaking to His disciples who were all still under the old covenant. Jesus hadn't yet died and risen so He was speaking to them before He went to the cross. God's kingdom, however, came on the day of Pentecost when the Holy Spirit was poured out into the hearts of every believer. Do you know what this means? It means that as new covenant, post-cross believers, God's kingdom has already come and is present on the inside of every one of us!

How To Release Kingdom Power

How can we reach a sick, broken and hurting world if we are sick, broken or hurting ourselves? We need to learn to live in the fullness of God's kingdom so that we can see God's kingdom power released—not only to reach and save the lost by preaching and demonstrating the gospel, but also to transform our own lives.

> Now to Him who is able to do exceedingly abundantly above all that we ask or think, **according to the power that works in us**, to Him be glory in the church by Christ Jesus to all generations, forever and ever. Amen.
>
> —Ephesians 3:20–21, NKJV

Did you get that? God is able to do anything, BUT it is according to God's power that is **at work within us**! But how do we draw on this power? The apostle Paul gives us the key:

> In conclusion, be strong in the Lord [be empowered **through your union** with Him]; **draw your strength** from Him [that strength which His boundless might provides].
>
> —Ephesians 6:10, AMP

We are empowered when we draw strength from God's indwelling Spirit. God is not a distant, impersonal energy or force. He is a loving heavenly Father who wants us to experience the fullness of His love that has already been shed abroad in our hearts (Romans 5:5, Ephesians 3:14–19). Through our faith in Jesus we already have union and have become one with Him, so through this relationship we can both experience and minister in God's boundless power.

> I have strength for all things in Christ **who empowers me** [I am ready for anything and equal to anything **through Him who infuses inner strength into me**; I am self-sufficient in Christ's sufficiency].
>
> —Philippians 4:13, AMP

As we spend time with God's indwelling Spirit, through both meditating on His Word and fellowshipping with Him, we will discover the truth of who He is, how to hear His voice and how to operate in the things of His kingdom. He will guide us into all truth, remind us of, and reveal to us what Jesus did and said, and lead us into victory!

Begin To Release God's Kingdom Power!

Now that you know that God's kingdom power is already within you, it is time to start releasing it. Remember that:

- God's kingdom now lives in us!
- We HAVE BEEN given the fullness of Christ (Colossians 2:9–10).
- We have the POWER to change.
- We have the POWER to live a life worth living.
- We have everything we need within us to rule and reign in this life with Christ.
- We belong to a supernatural kingdom!
- We can live a VICTORIOUS life in Christ!

So what is stopping you? God's righteousness, peace and joy are resident within you as is His nature, power and ability. Therefore, start walking by the truth of who you are in Christ and by what you have already inherited to see His power transform all areas of your life NOW!

The Foundations For Transforming Your Life

God Is Good—All The Time!

FOUR

"For the eyes of the Lord run to and fro throughout the whole earth, to **show Himself strong** in the behalf of them whose heart is perfect towards Him" (2 Chronicles 16:9, KJV).

I believe that the key to seeing God's power released in your life is not just about knowing what God has provided and how to apply it to your life, but also about knowing who He is to you personally. We need to come to the place where we KNOW that God is good—all the time! He is our loving heavenly Father and when you know this truth and you begin to see Him in this light, then your relationship with Him can be strengthened.

We begin this wonderful journey through Jesus. He is our entry point to a relationship with God the Father. The moment we put our faith in Jesus, our relationship with the Father began and through this relationship we can now come boldly and freely into the throne room of grace to obtain mercy in our time of need (Hebrews 4:15–16).

We are all at different levels in our walk with the Lord and we may all have different perceptions of who He is. If we have had poor examples of earthly parents then this can shape our view of God and the expectations we have of Him. Any flawed perspective can prevent us from walking in what He has freely provided. If we judge God through the experiences of our upbringing, we can easily limit His unconditional love and power and reduce it to a poor earthly example. Therefore, how we view God is crucial because it can affect how we relate to Him and how we are able to receive what He has freely provided through His Son.

We also need to be careful that we don't judge who God is or His will for our lives through the filter of our past experiences or through our natural understanding. If, for example, we feel angry, rejected, cheated, abandoned, or that we are going through some trial because God is trying to teach us something, then this incorrect view will prevent us from believing that God is good. Instead, we need to measure who God is through His Word and not by what we experience.

God does not use adverse circumstances to discipline, rebuke, test or tempt us. He disciplines, rebukes and corrects His children through His Word. Some falsely believe that the bad things that happen in life come from God, so they end up submitting to the natural circumstances rather than resisting them. But God does not test or tempt us with evil in any way.

> When tempted, no one should say, "God is tempting me." For God cannot be tempted by evil, nor does he tempt anyone; but each one is tempted when, by his own evil desire, he is dragged away and enticed. Then, after desire has conceived, it gives birth to sin; and sin, when it is full-grown, gives birth to death. **Don't be deceived**, my dear brothers. Every good and perfect gift is from above, coming down from the Father of the heavenly lights, who does not change like shifting shadows.
>
> —James 1:13–17

The Bible does talk about trials and temptations in life, but when taken in context the scriptures are not referring to our natural circumstances, but to the persecution that we may face in spreading the gospel. It is also our faith in Jesus that is tested, but this comes from the world and the adversary, not from God!

Jesus told us clearly in John 10:10 that all the lying, killing, stealing and destroying in life comes from the thief, the devil—not God! Jesus came to give us life and life abundantly. Therefore, we need to filter what we experience in life through this truth so that we know what is of the nature and character of the enemy and what is of the nature and character of God. It is through His Word that we discover what His will is and that His nature and character are always good, constant and unchanging.

> …"The Lord is upright; he is my Rock, and there is **no wickedness** in him."
>
> —Psalm 92:15

> This is the message we have heard from him and declare to you: **God is light**; in him there is **no darkness** at all.
>
> —1 John 1:5

God Is Love!

The Bible tells us in 1 John 4:8, 16 that "God is love". His love conquers all, covers a multitude of sins and never fails or wears out. He is patient and kind, He does not enforce His own way and He is ready to believe the best in every person (1 Corinthians 13, AMP). God loves us so much that He sent His only son to die for us so that we can have a relationship with Him for all eternity. But there is more! He doesn't want us to just know that He loves us, but He also wants us to experience His love.

> May Christ through your faith [actually] dwell (settle down, abide, make His permanent home) in your hearts! May you be rooted deep in love and founded securely on love, that you may have the power and be strong to apprehend and grasp with all the saints [God's

> devoted people, **the experience of that love**] what is the breadth and length and height and depth [of it]; [that you may really come] to know [practically, **through experience for yourselves**] the love of Christ, which far surpasses mere knowledge [without experience]; that you may be filled [through all your being] unto all the fullness of God [may have the richest measure of the divine Presence, and become a body **wholly filled** and flooded with God Himself]!
>
> —Ephesians 3:17–19, amp

Nothing in creation can ever separate us from the love of God (Romans 8:38–39). We need to know and renew our minds with the truth: God is a God of unconditional love who longs to have a daily living and growing relationship with us. He is not sitting on the throne ruling with an iron fist waiting for us to slip up so that He can punish us. No! Jesus took the punishment we deserved on the cross so that we now have His forgiveness, acceptance and unconditional love.

> How great is the love the Father has lavished on us, that we should be called children of God! And that is what we are...
>
> —1 John 3:1

God is a loving heavenly Father. In fact, He loves us so much that He has even numbered the hairs on our head.

> Indeed, the very hairs of your head are all numbered. Don't be afraid; you are worth more than many sparrows.
>
> —Luke 12:7

> How precious and weighty also are Your thoughts to me, O God! How vast is the sum of them! If I could count them, they would be more in number than the sand...
>
> —Psalm 139:17–18, amp

I encourage you to grow in your relationship with the Father by getting to know His unchanging nature and character through meditating on scriptures that outline His goodness, faithfulness and love. Spend time in fellowship with Him until this truth comes alive and you know for yourself that He is always good!

God Is The Giver Of Good Gifts

> Every good and perfect gift is from above, coming down from the Father of the heavenly lights, **who does not change** like shifting shadows.
>
> —James 1:17

God does not lie or change His mind. When He says something He always means it!

> God is not a man, that He should lie, nor a son of man, that He should change His mind. Does He speak and then not act? Does He promise and not fulfil?
>
> —Numbers 23:19

> a faith and knowledge resting on the hope of eternal life, which God, **who does not lie**, promised before the beginning of time.
>
> —Titus 1:2

God remains the same. Therefore, if He is the giver of good gifts one day, He is still the giver of good gifts the next. Depression, anxiety, fear, anger, jealousy, confusion, guilt, phobias, shame, sickness, disease, infertility and pain are not good gifts. They never were and they never will be! Through Jesus, God has made provision for His children to walk in health and wholeness. And the good news is that God will never withhold or withdraw what His Word promises or what He has already freely given to us through His Son.

> For God's gifts and His call are irrevocable. [He never withdraws them when once they are given, and He does not change His mind about those to whom He gives His grace or to whom He sends His call.]
>
> —Romans 11:29, amp

The Message translation of this verse says that "God's gifts and God's call are under full warranty—never cancelled, never rescinded". God is for you not against you (Romans 8:31), which means that He is on your side!

And His plans are always to prosper you, not to harm you, and to give you hope and a future (Jeremiah 29:11).

> The lions may grow weak and hungry, but those who seek the Lord lack no good thing.
>
> —Psalm 34:10

> …no good thing will He withhold from those who walk uprightly.
>
> —Psalm 84:11, NKJV

> "Which of you, if his son asks for bread, will give him a stone? Or if he asks for a fish, will give him a snake? If you, then, though you are evil, know how to give good gifts to your children, how much more will your Father in heaven give good gifts to those who ask him!"
>
> —Matthew 7:9–11 (Luke 11:11–13)

It is also important to note that God does not show partiality or favouritism (Acts 10:34, Romans 2:11), which means that He does not bless one person over another. His gifts are freely available to all who believe in Him. Everyone who calls on the name of the Lord will be saved—forgiven, healed, delivered, prospered, set free and made whole (Romans 10:11–13).

God Is Faithful

We have just discovered that it is through God's Word that we obtain knowledge of His will, nature and character. However, sometimes, we can become so focused on the Word that we begin to place more attention on the promises instead of on the One who gave us the promises! Let's look at the example of Abraham:

> By faith Abraham, even though he was past age—and Sarah herself was barren—was enabled to become a father because **he considered Him faithful who had made the promise**. And so from this one man, and he as good as dead, came descendants as numerous as the stars in the sky and as countless as the sand on the seashore.
>
> —Hebrews 11:11–12

It wasn't through Abraham's faith alone that he became a father despite the natural circumstances; he didn't consider the promise itself but, instead, considered the character of the One who made the promise.

In the passage quoted, verse 11 in the KJV translation says, "Through faith also **Sara herself received strength to conceive seed**, and was delivered of a child when she was past age, **because she judged Him faithful** who had promised."

And just like Sarah, when you consider that God is faithful, and that what He says is true, it will enable you to lay hold of the strength of God to see His power released to change your natural circumstances!

> ...the word of the Lord came to Abram in a vision, saying, "Do not be afraid, Abram. **I am your shield**, your **exceedingly great reward**."
>
> —Genesis 15:1, NKJV

God is OUR REWARD! Our reward is not the breakthrough or even the answer to our prayer. So our focus should be on Him. Remember that God has given you His very best— He gave you HIMSELF. He gave you Jesus. We have everything we need in Him!

> ...If God is for us, who can be against us? He who did not spare His own Son, but gave Him up for us all—how will He not also, **along with Him**, graciously give us all things?
>
> —Romans 8:31–32

Let Jesus be your provision! He is *Jehovah Jireh*, your provider, He is your righteousness, your peace, your healing and your reward! In Him is where you will find your breakthrough. He is the author and perfecter of your faith! Renew your mind with the truth that God is faithful and He will never leave you.

> ...be satisfied with your present [circumstances and with what you have]; for He [God] Himself has said, I will not in any way fail you nor give you up nor leave you without support. [I will] not, [I will]

> not, [I will] not in any degree leave you helpless nor forsake nor let you down (relax My hold on you)! [Assuredly not!] So we take comfort and are encouraged and confidently and boldly say, The Lord is my Helper; I will not be seized with alarm [I will not fear or dread or be terrified]. What can man do to me?
>
> —Hebrews 13:5–6, amp

Therefore seek Him first, worship Him, delight yourself in Him and remember always that…

> …no matter how many **promises** God has made, **they are "Yes" in Christ**. And so through Him the "Amen" ["so be it"] is spoken by us to the glory of God.
>
> —2 Corinthians 1:20, amp

The Word Of God

FIVE

"The unfolding of Your words gives light; it gives understanding to the simple" (Psalm 119:130).

Sadly, there is a lot of confusion when it comes to God's Word. Many misinterpret or do not understand what the Word is saying so they don't gain the full benefit from the promises and provision it contains. God's Word is not just a history book or a collection of stories. It is a book of life! And when you take the time to digest the message of what the words are saying, that is when the Word comes alive and becomes real and personal. This is how we begin to see God's power released in our lives! The Bible will, however, remain just a book and empty words on a page if it sits on your bookshelf unread, or if you don't allow yourself the time to meditate on it and understand what it is saying.

> The Spirit can make life. Sheer muscle and willpower don't make anything happen. Every word I've spoken to you is a Spirit-word, and so it is life-making [the NIV says…The words I have spoken to you are spirit and they are life].
>
> —John 6:63, The Message

The Bible is the source whereby God's power can transform your whole life. However, if you read God's Word regarding your situation and you don't comprehend what it says, then it will not be of any benefit to you. It is important then, to spend time meditating on what the Word says until it transforms from mere information into something real, personal and a source of life to you!

God's Word Is Our Instruction Book For Life!

> Your word is a lamp to my feet and a light for my path.
>
> —Psalm 119:105

The way God guides, leads, corrects, trains, equips, disciplines, rebukes and teaches us is by His Word.

> All Scripture is inspired by God and is useful to teach us what is true and to make us realize what is wrong in our lives. It corrects us when we are wrong and teaches us to do what is right. God uses it to prepare and equip His people to do every good work.
>
> —2 Timothy 3:16–17, NLT

God does not use adverse circumstances to discipline, rebuke, test or tempt us. Instead, as we have already seen, He corrects us through His Word. Remember, only good and perfect gifts come from God and He does not change (James 1:17).

> For the word of God is living and active. Sharper than any double-edged sword, it penetrates even to dividing soul and spirit, joints and marrow; it judges the thoughts and attitudes of the heart.
>
> —Hebrews 4:12

The Amplified Bible puts it this way: "For the word that God speaks is alive and full of power [making it active, operative, energizing, and effective]; it is sharper than any two-edged sword, penetrating to the dividing line of the breath of life (soul) and [the immortal] spirit, and of joints and marrow [of the deepest parts of our nature], exposing and sifting and analysing and judging the very thoughts and purposes of the heart."

We need to allow the truth of what God's Word says to overthrow our wrong attitudes and thoughts so that our minds can be renewed and our lives transformed.

God's Word Is Eternal Truth

Even though the Bible was completed nearly 2,000 years ago, God's Word is still relevant for us today. In fact, His Word will remain this way for all eternity.

> Heaven and earth will pass away, but my words will never pass away.
>
> —Matthew 24:35

> "...the word of the Lord stands forever."
>
> —1 Peter 1:25

God's Word is eternal. It is the same today as it was when it was first spoken or written. God does not change and it is impossible for Him to lie (Hebrews 6:18). So if His Word says that "by Jesus' stripes you have been healed" and that "you are blessed and prosperous", then this is exactly what it means!

Not only is God's Word our instruction book to demonstrate how we should live our lives, it also reveals the very nature and character of God, and details our new covenant with Him. It also reveals to us who we are in Christ, where we are seated and what belongs to us as His children. Most importantly, it tells us how to walk in the truth and see that truth become a reality in our lives.

> Sanctify them by the truth; your word is truth.
>
> —John 17:17

I have such a passion for God's Word. The more I grow in what His Word says, the more I grow in my relationship with Him. After all, His Word is all about Him! His Word has become the foundation of my life. For years, I lived in ignorance of the truth, but when I discovered the provision in His Word and acted on it, that truth set me free! Every breakthrough I have received is the result of taking God at His Word and applying what that Word said to my life.

This began when my husband, Shaun, was diagnosed as sterile and told that we could never have children. I meditated on the truth of what God's Word said until it became personal to me. I then learnt to walk by what that Word said and not by what the natural facts were and the result was four children in four years! I have since learnt to apply the truth found in God's Word to every other area and I have continued to see victory in many areas of my life.

God's Word Is Already Established!

God's Word will stand true forever because He has already established His Word and covenant here on earth. Every provision within it is signed and sealed by the blood of Jesus. This means that His Word and covenant cannot be altered or broken because it wasn't made between God and men, but between God and Himself (Hebrews 6:13–18). When we accepted Christ's sacrifice on the cross, we came into relationship with God and entered into this covenant. We became God's own children and joint heirs with Christ (Galatians 4:7, Romans 8:17). This means that everything Jesus purchased for us is now our inheritance. And within our inheritance is provision for both this life and for the one to come. All that God has done now belongs to us. Through Jesus, He took our sin, sickness, pain, shame, lack and loss. He forgave us, justified us and gave us His health, love, acceptance, fruitfulness and prosperity in every area of our lives. Sounds like a great exchange to me!

What I also find exciting is that God does not show favouritism by choosing certain people to bless; His blessings are for ALL who are in relationship with Him. This means that God does not choose to bless some of His children and not others, or to heal some and not others. What Jesus purchased has already been established so God cannot withhold from us or deny us what He has already freely provided. So while all our circumstances differ from one another, one thing that will remain constant and unchanging is what God has already established for us as outlined in His Word.

> For where there is a [last] will and testament involved, the death of the one who made it must be established, for a will and testament is valid and takes effect only at death, since it has no force or legal power as long as the one who made it is alive.
>
> —Hebrews 9:16–17, amp

If our earthly parents died and left us possessions in a will then we wouldn't have to wait for, ask, pray, beg or plead for them. Those possessions would now belong to us—*we would have inherited them.* We would simply need to go and take possession of our new belongings. And it is the same with our godly inheritance. We don't need to ask for what already belongs to us, we simply possess and enjoy what God has already freely provided.

> My covenant will I **not break**, nor alter the thing that is gone out of My lips.
>
> —Psalm 89:34, kjv

God's Word is His will and testament to us! God has bound Himself to His Word. He swore by Himself, so it can never be broken (Isaiah 45:23 and Hebrews 6:13). All of the provisions within our covenant are set out in God's Word. Every area of life is covered, so if you want to know what God's will is for a particular area of your life, then search His Word to see what it says. If God said it, then you can believe that He meant it!

While a lot of God's promises and blessings are mainly revealed in the Old Testament, they are not exclusive to those under the old covenant

(Deuteronomy 28:1–14). God's plans and purposes for His children remain the same for us today! Yet, some dispute that Christians can claim these old covenant blessings because they believe that the blessings are no longer relevant. But why would God not want us to continue to be blessed in the same areas that Abraham and his descendants were?

These blessings are still God's plan because Genesis 17:7 says that the covenant that God made with Abraham was for his descendants and also for the generations to come. Genesis 12:3 also says that all peoples on the earth will be blessed through Abraham and Galatians 3:29 says, "If you belong to Christ, then you are Abraham's seed, and heirs according to the promise." Galatians 3:6–9 not only reinforces this, but also states that those who are of faith will be blessed along with Abraham! So it's plain to see that as "Abraham's seed and heirs according to the promise", we are entitled to receive the Old Testament blessings.

Consider also that if God's plan was different for the new covenant believer, then that would mean that God had changed His mind and will for mankind. But we know that God does not change (Malachi 3:6). He is the same today as He was yesterday and He will remain the same forever (Hebrews 13:8). We also know that only good gifts come from Him because He is our Father and even earthly fathers know how to give good gifts to their children (Luke 11:13).

As believers in Jesus Christ, we have a better covenant based on better promises than the old covenant (Hebrews 8:6). In fact, Jesus was the fulfilment of all the promises and blessings in the old covenant through His death, burial and resurrection. He reversed the curse and paid the price for all forms of sickness and disease, poverty, debts, lack, shame, pain and everything else that entered the world through sin. This means that the price has been paid in full. So the same blessings of health, provision, prosperity and fruitfulness in the old covenant are still God's will for His children and remain the same truth for us today.

God's Will Is What His Word Says!

In Hosea 4:6, God says, "My people are destroyed from lack of knowledge..." This scripture is talking about God's people being destroyed, or suffering through not knowing or understanding who He is and what He has provided. If we don't know what God's will is for our lives then we won't know what is available to us. But we don't have to be in the dark concerning the will of God for our lives. His will and plan for us always remain clear and constant. Why? Because God's will for our lives is found within His Word! Any one of us can therefore discover God's will, plan and purpose for our lives by reading through the pages of our Bible.

> This is the confidence we have in approaching God: that if we ask anything according to His will, He hears us. And if we know that He hears us - whatever we ask - we know that we have what we asked of Him.
>
> —1 John 5:14–15

Whatever is in God's Word is His will for your life—and in His Word is provision for every area of your life. You can always rely on God's Word because it has already been established. So God's will for you isn't what the doctors say, what your symptoms say, what your diagnosis is, what your bank balance is or what the natural circumstances dictate; but rather what His Word says!

There may be times in our lives when our circumstances don't line up with the Word, and we may conclude that what happened was God's will for that situation. But we need to realise that God's Word isn't proven or disproven by our personal experiences. When our circumstances don't line up with what the Word says, we shouldn't judge or assume it is God's will or plan or that He is withholding from us. Instead, we should continue to uphold God's Word as the final authority—not our circumstances, and when we live by that truth we can then start to see what it says become reality in our lives.

When our circumstances speak contrary to what is in God's Word, it can be due to any number of reasons. But we can be certain that it was never because it is God's will—as He cannot act contrary to His own Word. God will never break His Word—ever! He has sworn by Himself so we can be confident that He will always keep His promises.

Does God Still 'Watch His Word'?

> The Lord said to me, "You have seen correctly, for I am watching to see that My word is fulfilled." [The NKJV says...for I am ready to perform My word.]
>
> —Jeremiah 1:12

In the Old Testament, when God spoke, He saw to it that His words would be fulfilled. His words never failed or returned empty, but accomplished what He desired and achieved the purpose for which He sent them (Isaiah 55:11). In fact, what God spoke or promised was just like a legal contract because He doesn't say one thing and then do another. He cannot lie, change His mind or deceive us (Hebrews 6:16–18).

> "Therefore say to them, 'This is what the Sovereign Lord says: None of My words will be delayed any longer; whatever I say will be fulfilled, declares the Sovereign Lord.'"
>
> —Ezekiel 12:28

Much of what God promised in the old covenant was pointing to what He would do through Jesus on the cross. So while the old covenant looked forward to what the cross would accomplish, as new covenant believers, we now look back at what the cross **has already accomplished**! That means that for you and I, God has **already performed** His word through Jesus. He is the living Word of God. So when it comes to what is already established in God's Word and what He has already performed through His Son, it is no longer a promise **but rather a provision**. This is why ALL of the promises of God are "yes" and "Amen" (so be it) in Christ (2 Corinthians 1:20). So when we discover what God has provided through Christ, we don't need to pray, ask or wait for God to perform His Word in our lives. Why? Because **He has already** sent forth His Word and healed us, and forgiven, blessed, prospered, delivered and set us free from sin and death, sickness and disease, and from all the power of the enemy—past tense.

God's Word Is His Seed

In Matthew 13:1–52, Mark 4:1–32 and Luke 8:4–15, Jesus shares several parables on how God's kingdom operates. He compares natural seed with God's Word. In Luke 8:11, it states that the seed that produces God's kingdom is the Word of God. In talking about seeds, Jesus used something that the people of that day understood. It was a simple yet powerful analogy of how God's kingdom (His nature, power and ability) comes, grows and outworks in our lives.

In the natural earthly realm, God created plants to reproduce after themselves through the growth and germination of seeds. A seed already has everything created within it to reproduce after its own kind, so when the seed is planted, it will come to life, grow and bear fruit. In like manner, EVERYTHING has already been programmed into the seed of God's Word so that when it is sown, ALL BY ITSELF, it will come to life, grow and bear fruit in your life!

> ...This is what the kingdom of God is like. A man scatters seed on the ground. Night and day, whether he sleeps or gets up, the seed sprouts and grows, though he does not know how.
>
> —Mark 4:26–27

I recently watched a documentary on Egypt. It showed how wheat seed was found in the pyramids. The seeds were dated to approximately 2,500BC. Incredibly, when the seeds were planted in fertile soil, the 4,500-year-old seeds grew! In the same way, God's Word does not lose potency over time, but continues to powerfully reproduce His kingdom in the lives of those who have sown it. Therefore, when the truth of God's timeless Word is planted in the fertile soil of our hearts, His kingdom power will come to life and grow.

No Seed Planted Means No Harvest!

No farmer can expect a harvest without first having planted the seeds! Have you ever looked at an unplanted seed? It appears dead, shrivelled and lifeless before being planted. But when sown into fertile soil, all by itself the seed will sprout and grow. However, if the seed is not planted into fertile soil, the seed remains dormant and will not come to life and reproduce. Because there is already life in the seed, the process of the seed coming to life is not dependant on God, but on the seed being planted and the condition of the ground it is sown into.

> As the rain and the snow come down from heaven, and do not return to it without watering the earth and making it bud and flourish, so that it yields seed for the sower and bread for the eater, so is My word that goes out from My mouth: It will not return to Me empty, but will accomplish what I desire and achieve the purpose for which I sent it.
>
> —Isaiah 55:10–11

Plant—Don't Scatter—The Seed!

It is important to note that we do not just "grab" a scripture and simply declare it or "throw it" at our circumstances—like scattering seed into thin air—and then expect that this will magically change things. While God's Word is alive and full of power, we need to remember the principle of how a seed works. Seeds only come to life and start producing when they are planted in fertile soil—not thrown into thin air. In the same way, God's Word comes to life when it is planted in the fertile soil within our hearts. We are the ground where the Word needs to be sown (not sown in our outward circumstances) because God's Word needs to become living and active in us!

It is also important to mention that simply declaring God's Word "by rote" can be ineffective and powerless. Instead, we need to understand the message of what the words are saying. If we want to see what God's Word says come to pass in our lives, then it is not about *throwing it* at our circumstances, but about *sowing it* into our hearts. How do we do that? By spending time meditating on what it says until the message comes alive and we understand what it is saying to us personally.

> ...faith comes by hearing, and hearing by the word of God.
>
> —Romans 10:17, NKJV

Faith comes from hearing about what Jesus has done! Seeing the fullness of what we have inherited upon salvation outworking in our lives comes the same way. We don't need to keep hearing the Word to get more faith because when we believed in Jesus, we received the fullness of who He is. Instead, we need to keep hearing about what Jesus has done so that we can know what we have already inherited!

How Does The Word Grow?

> ...in a humble (gentle, modest) spirit receive and welcome the word **which implanted and rooted** [in your hearts] contains the power to save your souls.
>
> —James 1:21, AMP

In the scripture above, "implanted" literally means engrafted—when something foreign becomes a part of whatever it is grafted onto. Strong's Concordance describes the word "engrafted" as "to swell up; to germinate or grow (sprout, produce), literally or figuratively, to spring up"! Therefore, it is important that you spend time in God's Word until it is engrafted in your heart, so that it can spring to life, take root and grow. You do this by transforming your thinking through renewing your mind with the truth of what the Word says regarding your situation, until that truth springs up and becomes more real to you than what the natural circumstances are saying.

Initially, for many of us, the natural circumstances may appear more real and powerful than the truth found in God's Word, but the natural report doesn't need to be our final report! When we continue to meditate on what God's Word says instead of what the natural is doing, then we are giving the Word a chance to transform the way we think and how we see our situation. This process is vital as it enables the seed of God's Word to spring to life, grow, develop, take root and bear fruit. Then, we will start seeing our lives with what God's Word says rather than without it. That way, if we are challenged, we won't easily lose sight of the truth because once the Word has been "engrafted", it has already become a part of our thinking. We then put the Word into practice by acting on it to start experiencing what it says.

Seeing God's Word grow in our lives is two-fold: We need to allow God's Word to grow in us, and then we need to grow up in the Word! Jesus said that we should not live on bread alone, but on every Word that comes from the mouth of God (Matthew 4:4). We need to stop feeding on the things of this world and start feeding and chewing on what the Word says so that our minds are renewed and our lives transformed from the inside out.

> as newborn babes, desire the pure milk of the word, that you may grow thereby. [The nlt says…Like newborn babies, you must crave pure spiritual milk so that **you will grow** into a **full experience** of salvation. Cry out for this nourishment.]
>
> —1 Peter 2:2, nkjv

God wants us to experience the fullness of His salvation! The word "salvation" in this scripture in Greek means, to be saved, delivered, healed and made whole. God's salvation is not just about the forgiveness of sins and inheriting eternal life because what Jesus purchased for us on the cross is for every area of life including the here and now.

God's Word Brings Increase!

The condition of the ground plays an important role in the healthy germination of a seed. In the same way, the condition of the "soil" of our heart is vitally important for the growth of the seed of God's Word. The Bible says that "in a humble (gentle, modest) spirit" we are to "receive and welcome the word" (James 1:21, amp). If the message of the seed of God's Word is not understood, hits "stony" or "hard ground", or is "sown among thorns" (the cares of the world), it will not come to life, take root, grow and bear fruit in our lives (Mark 4:3–8, 13–20). Jesus shares this in Matthew 13, Mark 4 and Luke 8 in the parable of the sower. In these passages, He mentioned four different conditions of the ground and what happens when the seed is sown in those conditions:

> And He said to them, "Do you not understand this parable? How then will you understand all the parables? The sower **sows the word.** And these are the ones by the wayside where the word is sown. When they hear, **Satan comes immediately** and takes away the word that was sown in their hearts. These likewise are the ones sown on **stony ground** who, when they hear the word, immediately receive it with gladness; and they **have no root** in themselves, and so endure only for a time. Afterward, when tribulation or persecution arises **for the word's sake**, immediately they stumble. Now these are the ones **sown among thorns**; they are the ones who hear the word, and the cares of this world, the deceitfulness of riches, and the desires for other things entering in choke the word, and it becomes unfruitful. But these are the ones sown on **good ground**, those who **hear the word, accept it, and bear fruit**: some thirtyfold, some sixty, and some a hundred."
>
> —Mark 4:13–20, NKJV

1. **No understanding**—those who hear the Word and don't understand it give Satan the opportunity to come immediately and snatch the Word from their hearts. Matthew 13:19, NKJV, says it this way: "When anyone hears the word of the kingdom, **and does not understand it**, then the wicked one comes and snatches away what was sown in his heart".

2. **Stony ground**—those who hear the Word and at first receive it with gladness, BUT because they don't allow the Word to develop roots, they stumble and let go of the Word when temptation, tribulation and persecution comes, or when the natural circumstances are too overwhelming.

3. **Seed sown among thorns**—those who allow the cares of the world, deceitfulness of riches and the desires for other things to come in and choke the Word, making it become unfruitful.

4. **Good ground**—those who hear the Word, understand what it says, accept and live in its truth, enabling the seed to come to life, take root, grow and bear fruit in abundance!

This is the process where everything within God's kingdom comes and grows in our lives and when His Word becomes living and active in us. Jesus is the living Word of God that became flesh and dwelt among us (John 1:1–2, 14). When the message of the gospel of Jesus is sown in people's hearts and they believe and receive it, it brings LIFE—abundant life, resurrection life and eternal life! The fullness of what Jesus purchased through the finished work of the cross comes and grows the same way.

Satan Comes For The Word

Satan wants to exalt himself (and his works) and appear more powerful than Jesus in your mind. His greatest weapon is to keep you ignorant of the truth so that you don't live out of what God says about who you are in Christ and your position in Him. You will then end up submitting to the situation or to Satan's lies rather than resisting him and exercising your God-given power and authority in the situation.

Satan will tell you that God's Word is not true and will remind you of all your past failures. He wants you trapped in the natural realm by keeping your focus on the natural, so that you become overwhelmed by the circumstances. Your symptoms or circumstances may even get worse. You may also feel weak and too tired to do anything. But stop walking by sight, feelings and appearances and start walking by faith—by the truth of what God's Word says. Remember always that even though we may be physically and emotionally exhausted, the truth is that our Spirit is always strong because we have the same Spirit of Jesus dwelling on the inside of us! And because He dwells in us, we always have access to His nature, love, strength, power and might. He never sleeps nor slumbers, so He is always awake, always willing, and always able to come and help and guide us in our time of need, and lead us into triumphant victory!

How To Receive Revelation From God's Word

When we read God's Word, we can't simply pick out a scripture that sounds good and say to ourselves, "Yes, I'll have that," and leave it there. We begin with that, but in order to have what that scripture says become a reality in our lives, we need to receive a personal revelation. The truth of what that Word says needs to progress from being simple "head knowledge", that is, an intellectual understanding of God's Word in our minds, to "heart knowledge", which is **revelation** of what the Word is saying (the message within the Word) to us personally.

Psalm 119:130, KJV tells us that "The entrance of thy words giveth light; it giveth understanding unto the simple". When God's Word enters **and finds its place in us**, it brings light, life and revelation. So we need to spend time meditating on the truth of what God's Word says until **information** becomes **revelation.**

> Counsel in the heart of man is like deep water, but a man of **understanding** will draw it out.
>
> —Proverbs 20:5, NKJV

> My mouth shall speak wisdom, and the **meditation** of my heart shall give understanding.
>
> —Psalm 49:3, NKJV

For some, to have the truth in God's Word established in their hearts is a simple process, whereas for others, it can take time for revelation to be realised. Today, we live in a "microwave" society. We don't want to wait for anything; we want it now! But it takes time to overcome fear and doubt and renew our mind with the truth of what God has said in His Word. Sometimes, the natural circumstances can also overwhelm us so it can take time for God's Word to become real, personal and deeply rooted in us. Therefore, it may take some persistence on our part to meditate on God's truth until it comes to life and transforms our thinking.

Now, when I say "meditate", I am referring to biblical meditation and not that which is associated with Eastern philosophies or religions. In Hebrew, the word "meditate" literally means to immerse your whole self in the truth of what the Word says by picturing, pondering, imagining, studying and musing it over within your mind and inner man, while also muttering, uttering and speaking this truth to yourself with the words of your mouth. We read earlier that Joshua was instructed not to let God's Word depart from his mouth, but to meditate on it day and night so that he could observe himself doing all that it said. This was the key to how Joshua would become prosperous and have good success (Joshua 1:8, NKJV). God also tells us in Proverbs 4:20 to incline our ears to His Word, not let it depart from our sight and to keep and guard it in our hearts, because His Word is life to those who find them and healing and health to our flesh and outward circumstances. Meditating on the Word, therefore, is not meant to be a one-off occurrence, but rather it needs to be continued until you are able to see your circumstances through the eyes of God's Word instead of what you can only see and understand in the natural realm.

Another reason we need to spend time meditating on the Word is so that the Holy Spirit can reveal and help bring the Word to life.

> [For I always pray to] the God of our Lord Jesus Christ, the Father of glory, that He may grant you a **spirit of wisdom and revelation** [of insight into mysteries and secrets] in the [deep and intimate] **knowledge of Him**, by having the **eyes of your heart flooded with light**, so that you can **know and understand** the hope to which He has called you, and how rich is His glorious inheritance in the saints (His set-apart ones), and [so that you can **know and understand**] what is the immeasurable and unlimited and surpassing greatness of His power in and for us who believe...
>
> —Ephesians 1:17–19, AMP

The Holy Spirit will bring the revelation and understanding you need to know God more intimately. Therefore, we need to become more acquainted with His ways so that He can help us experience all that God has provided for us.

> But as it is written: "Eye has not seen, nor ear heard, nor have entered into the heart of man the things which God has prepared for those who love Him." **But God has revealed them to us through His Spirit**. For the Spirit searches all things, yes, the deep things of God. For what man knows the things of a man except the spirit of the man which is in him? Even so no one knows the things of God except the Spirit of God. Now we have received, not the spirit of the world, but **the Spirit who is from God,** that **we might know** the things that have been freely given to us by God.
>
> —1 Corinthians 2:9–12, nkjv

Amen! This is good news! But there is more...

> These things we also speak, not in words which man's wisdom teaches but which the Holy Spirit teaches, comparing spiritual things with spiritual. But the natural man does not receive the things of the Spirit of God, for they are foolishness to him; nor can he know them, **because they are spiritually discerned**. But he who is spiritual judges all things, yet he himself is rightly judged by no one. For "who has known the mind of the Lord that he may instruct Him?" But **we have the mind of Christ**.
>
> —1 Corinthians 2:13–16, nkjv

We have access to the very mind of Jesus. 1 John 2:20, kjv, says, "...ye have an unction from the Holy One, and **ye know all things**." Of course this is not speaking about our natural understanding because the reality is that we don't know everything. Instead, this scripture is talking about the mind of the Spirit of Christ who lives within us because He knows all things! Remember that Jesus is the exact representation of the Father (Hebrews 1:3, John 14:9–10). The Father, Spirit and Son are all one!

> A shoot [Jesus] will come up from the stump of Jesse; from his roots a Branch will bear fruit. The Spirit of the Lord will rest on him—the Spirit of **wisdom** and of **understanding**, the Spirit of **counsel** and of **power**, the Spirit of **knowledge** and of the fear of the Lord.
>
> —Isaiah 11:1–3

Jesus possesses all wisdom, understanding, knowledge, counsel, power and might! It stands to reason then, that if we need answers or solutions to what we face in life, we need to spend time in God's Word to gain wisdom, knowledge and understanding on what to do.

Revelation begins when our mind (natural thinking) discovers a truth that we read or hear in God's Word. The Holy Spirit agrees (brings an inner witness) and if we continue to embrace that truth, it becomes real and alive to us personally. We will begin to see things differently because our thinking has been transformed.

> The Spirit himself testifies with our spirit that we are God's children.
>
> —Romans 8:16

> …this is how we know that he lives in us: We know it by the Spirit he gave us.
>
> —1 John 3:24

> …it is the Spirit who bears witness, because the Spirit is truth.
>
> —1 John 5:6, NKJV

> He who believes in the Son of God has the witness in himself…
>
> —1 John 5:10, NKJV

> ...the Spirit will take from what is mine and make it known to you.
>
> —John 16:15

> The Spirit gives life; the flesh counts for nothing. The words I have spoken to you are spirit and they are life.
>
> —John 6:63

Spending time renewing our mind with what God's Word says is essential to get our natural mind (thinking, feelings and understanding) to agree with the Spirit (the mind of Christ). When we think in line with the Spirit, we also act in line with Him. This is how we see God's power "at work" within us to do superabundantly above and beyond what we can even ask, imagine or dream (Ephesians 3:20).

It Is Not About Following A Formula!

One of the questions I often get asked by people who are in a fix is, "What scripture can I claim for my situation?" I also get asked why, when people have prayed, believed and declared God's Word, nothing changed? But this is not what the Word is about. When you need a breakthrough, it is not about applying a method, naming and claiming a scripture or declaring out aloud what the Word says verbatim without any understanding. Applying a formula doesn't magically make something happen. When we are in a desperate situation, it is easy to get stuck applying formulas and getting into works and self-effort, which only leads to frustration. The Word is powerless without relationship! Stop applying formulas with the literal Word and instead get to know the living Word (Jesus). When you know the One who gave the Word, believing the Word is simple!

It is important to understand that declaring the Word is not about getting God to move, to do something for you or to make something happen. **The Word is there to show us what has already happened**! The Word reveals what Jesus purchased for us through the finished work of the cross and shows what has already been established. It is then our responsibility to take the information, renew our mind with it to transform the way we think, so that we can find the wisdom, revelation and understanding we need.

Revelation Brings Rest

If you are discouraged, frustrated or striving for your breakthrough, then you are not at rest. If this is where you are currently at, then I encourage you to sit down! By this, I mean to remember your position in God's kingdom—you are seated with Christ in heavenly places (Ephesians 2:6). When we received Jesus as our Saviour, we entered into His rest. The Christian life is not about do, do, do (our performance), but rather done, done, done (Jesus' performance)! Jesus has already done everything He could possibly do through the finished work of the cross. This is why, when Jesus ascended into heaven, He sat down. He has finished everything He came to do, so He is now seated and at rest with the Father. Likewise, we also need to cease from all our self-efforts, performance and works and rest in what Jesus has already provided for us. We begin by meditating on the truth of what Jesus has done until the revelation that produces rest comes!

When revelation and understanding come and you believe God's Word above all else, it positions you in that place of rest. You will find that any striving, hoping, begging or pleading and desperation will fade and disappear, because you will have come to a place where you know that God's Word is His will for you personally. The truth of what the Word says will then not be easily lost when you are challenged in that area. Nor will Satan be able to lie or deceive you anymore because you will know the truth for your situation. Then, you simply continue to act on what that truth says and soon the rest will be history!

How To Walk By Faith

SIX

Faith is an area where I often see Christians struggle—and I used to be one of them! Because of this, I now have a passion to teach the truth of the simplicity of faith and how it works. And let me assure you, faith is not meant to be a struggle!

There is so much teaching available on the subject of faith, some of which is unhelpful, condemning or confusing. However, when I discovered the truth about what faith is and how it worked, my life was radically transformed and I have seen amazing breakthroughs as a result.

What Is Faith?

Many believers have the wrong idea of what faith is. Unfortunately, their concept of faith is based upon their own ability to perform, so they get caught up in works and self-effort trying to get God to respond to their need. Faith has also been portrayed as something mysterious and unknown that we need to possess before God will act. But God doesn't expect us to just accept everything without any basis of understanding. Faith is not blind, and it is not based on the unknown.

The biblical definition of faith is straightforward. The Greek word for faith is *pistis* and it means trust, confidence or assurance. Vine's lexicon defines faith as "firm persuasion" and Thayer's lexicon defines it as "conviction of the truth of anything".

Faith is therefore based on facts—on something or someone known, and is built on trust! How we build trust in anyone is based on the character of the person. When we trust them, we have an assurance that what they say is true, so we expect what they say to come to pass. If, on the other hand, we don't know their character, then we won't be able to trust their words. But we can have confidence in God because His character, will and plan for mankind is known. They are established in His Word.

It is important to note that faith is not anchored in the natural realm, so it does not come from our natural feelings and emotions. We all exercise human faith every day, but when we have faith in God, we can move mountains! Human faith is based on what we relate to with our feelings and natural senses: hearing, sight, smell, taste or touch. Our faith in God, on the other hand, is spiritual and is based on what we don't see: the forgiveness of sins, our righteousness in God and everything contained within the spiritual realm of God's kingdom. To believe in a God that we cannot physically see means that we possess faith. And that faith was at work when we accepted Jesus Christ as our Lord and Saviour.

> ...faith comes from hearing the message, and the message is heard through the word of Christ.
>
> —Romans 10:17

Faith comes and grows from hearing about who Jesus is and what He has done! The day you became a Christian, you heard the Word of God (the message of Jesus) and faith came! In other words, the message was quickened (came alive) through the hearing of God's Word and you believed what it said. You then used that faith (belief) to accept Jesus' sacrifice and you received your salvation. As a result, you were born again (or made alive) by the Spirit of God.

Faith is simple! It is believing in who Jesus is and resting in what He has done! Our faith in Jesus is enough because when we believed in Him, we received everything we needed to live a victorious and blessed life—one that's worth living! And seeing the fullness of what we have inherited upon salvation outworking in our lives comes the same way. We don't need to keep hearing the Word to get more faith. Instead, we need to keep hearing so that we can discover what we already have!

> Praise be to the God and Father of our Lord Jesus Christ, **who has blessed us** in the heavenly realms **with every spiritual blessing** in Christ.
>
> —Ephesians 1:3

We have been given (past tense) every spiritual blessing in Christ. This is exciting because **the spiritual realm has the power to change the natural realm**! And when you understand how to apply this truth, you can see the manifestation of His power released to transform your life!

We All Have Faith!

When I first faced the impossible, natural situation of my husband Shaun's sterility, my first thought was that I lacked the faith I needed for our miracle, and so I found myself in a frenzy trying to muster faith out of thin air. The more attention I gave our natural circumstances, the more that faith appeared to be out of my reach. But as I spent time with God seeking Him for answers, He revealed the good news that faith was not only within my reach, but is also available to every believer. We all have faith. We just need to learn how to live and walk by it in our everyday life.

Here are some questions that I believe will demonstrate my point:

- Are you fully persuaded that you are a Christian and that when you die you will not perish but will have eternal life?
- Do you have any doubts about this?
- *Do you have any fears about this?*

When I asked these questions at one of my ministry meetings and also at the Healing School I lectured at, everyone was confidently able to say that they knew beyond any doubt that they have their salvation. Not one of them experienced doubts or fears about this. They were fully persuaded and knew that they were already saved. If anyone were to question, ridicule or persecute them, they knew that it would not move them from this belief, and I am sure that most of you who are reading this will have the same assurance.

If I ask similar questions to the ones above, but this time about healing, I wonder if I will receive the same answers.

- Are you fully persuaded that by Jesus' stripes you are healed?
- Do you have any doubts about this?
- *Do you have any fears about this?*

Many Christians do not realise that they already have faith and that they live and walk by faith every day of their lives. All they need to do is to have the same assurance for other areas of their lives as they do for their salvation. And this assurance comes when you know what Jesus has purchased through the finished work of the cross and what you have already inherited as a believer.

Romans 12:3, NKJV, tells us that we all have "a measure of faith" (the KJV says "**the** measure of faith"). This isn't saying that we all have different measures of faith, but rather, it is talking about "the measure" of faith it takes to receive salvation. It's the same measure, which means that for new covenant believers, it is no longer about someone having "big faith", "little faith" or "great faith". Instead, we need to use the faith that we already have. While it appears that some may have more faith than others, the reality is that we all have the same measure! This means that we all have the **same potential** to walk in the fullness of what Jesus died to give us and also the **same ability** to act on what we believe to see God's power released to change our lives and natural circumstances.

Let me explain it this way: It is not "by your faith" that you receive what you need, but **because you have faith** in Jesus, it means that **you have already received** all that you need! When you heard the message of Christ, you didn't have to build your faith to receive forgiveness of your sins, a relationship with God or eternal life, did you? No! When you believed in Jesus, **you received** forgiveness, relationship and eternal life! This is the same with everything that Jesus has purchased for us! For example, we don't need to build our faith to receive healing. Why? **Because of your faith in Jesus**, you **have** healing! Your faith in Jesus gives you the legal rights of an heir, which you received upon salvation. Through your faith in Jesus, **you have already obtained everything** you need in life. You simply need to renew your mind until you know this truth so that you can start embracing what belongs to you. So stop trying to get what is already yours and start believing and acting on the truth that you already have it!

Faith In The Old Covenant

In the Old Testament, those who believed God simply acted on what He had said because they expected Him to do what He had promised. Noah, Abraham, Moses and Joshua are great examples of this. They were not looking to the things that were seen but to the unseen so they acted on His Word before there was anything visible or tangible. In Hebrews 11, we read how they and many others believed and acted on God's Word even though their natural circumstances seemed contrary to what had been promised to them. They had nothing in the natural realm to base their faith on except God's Word. Their trust in Him and His Word enabled them to believe what He had promised.

In the Gospels, Jesus demonstrated God's kingdom with signs and wonders. Everywhere He went He opposed the devil's work by healing the sick, raising the dead, casting out devils, cleansing lepers, forgiving sins and preaching the good news of God's kingdom. He was the revelation and manifestation of the Father in action. There was nothing blind about the people's faith in Jesus. The people acted on what they heard and saw Him do. Some received from Him as He was passing by, others came to Him and requested help, and others came determined to receive what they needed. And we know that Jesus healed all who came to Him!

Faith In The New Covenant

One thing we need to remember when reading the Old Testament (old covenant) and the Gospels is that the people didn't have God's Spirit living in them like we do today. We live under a new covenant based on better promises, and we have the benefit of having His indwelling Spirit guide and teach us. They had Jesus in the flesh; we have the Spirit of Jesus living in us. We also have the Bible, which shows us who Jesus is and the fullness of what He has done. We don't need to see before we believe. We have evidence and proof of what has already been established all outlined in God's Word. Jesus said to Thomas, "...because you have seen me, you have believed. Blessed are those who have not seen and yet have believed" (John 20:29, NKJV).

Remember also that we are now post-cross, born again, Spirit-filled believers. We received His Spirit the day we put our faith in Jesus. When this took place, we received within ourselves the fullness of who Jesus is (Colossians 2:9–10). This means that everything that belongs to Jesus also belongs to us now.

- We are joint heirs with Christ (we have the same inheritance).
- We have the same Father and spiritual DNA.
- We have the same Spirit of power (Acts 1:8, Romans 8:11).

- We are seated with Christ in heavenly places (Ephesians 1:20; 2:6, NKJV).
- We have the same position in the kingdom, including His dominion, power and authority (see Chapter 8, Your Position In Christ).
- As Jesus is, so are we in this world (1 John 4:17, NKJV).

Do you realise what this means? We are no longer limited to our natural human abilities. Because we have faith in Jesus, we have the same Holy Spirit, and the same authority and power that Jesus used to heal the sick, raise the dead, cast out devils, calm storms and set captives free!

We Already Have What We Need!

I have had many people ask me to pray for them to receive more faith. I too, in the past, have had times when I felt that I needed more faith to overcome a particular situation. As we have just discovered, however, the reality is that we don't need more faith; we simply need to exercise the faith we already have!

We need to stop looking at ourselves and at "our faith", and start looking at Jesus and what He has done! If we know what we already have, then we don't need to work to earn what is already ours! The work Jesus did was a complete work and is freely available to all who believe in Him. We **already have the inheritance**; it is our possession so we might as well walk in it!

> The apostles said to the Lord, "**Increase our faith**!" He replied, "If you have faith as small as a mustard seed, **you can say** to this mulberry tree, 'Be uprooted and planted in the sea,' and it will obey you."
>
> —Luke 17:5–6

The apostles asked Jesus for more faith, but look at His reply: "If you have faith as small as a mustard seed you can say..." On the surface, this may seem like Jesus didn't answer their question, but the opposite is true. Jesus showed them how they didn't need to increase their faith, but instead they were to start using the faith they had! In the same way, we also need to look at using the faith we've already got.

There may be many of you who feel that you are struggling with faith. But be encouraged that it isn't a lack of faith that is the issue, but rather a lack of knowledge. However, this is easily resolved because God's Word gives you the knowledge you need for every area of life!

> His divine power **has given us everything we need** for life and godliness **through our knowledge of Him** who called us by His own glory and goodness. Through these **He has given us** His very **great and precious promises**, so that **through them** you may participate in the divine nature and escape the corruption in the world caused by evil desires.
>
> —2 Peter 1:3–4

Knowledge is an essential element to faith because we can't put our trust in someone or something we don't know. If we don't know what God's will is for our lives or if we don't know what Jesus purchased for us on the cross, then we won't know what is available. You may say, "I am just going to trust God." But what are you trusting Him to do? If you don't know what is available to you, then what substance or evidence are you putting your trust in? Is it based on a hunch, on feelings or on hope? Faith is not blind. Faith is tangible and is based on facts. God's Word is the substance and evidence that we can trust because it gives us knowledge, it is known and it shows us the facts!

Remember, if you are a believer in Jesus, then faith is already present because faith is simply believing in Him. For this reason, we don't meditate on God's Word to get more faith, but rather to receive knowledge, gain understanding and to obtain revelation of what we already have!

Saved By Grace Through Faith

To live in the fullness of our inheritance, we first need to know what Jesus purchased for us through the finished work of the cross so that we can start applying what we have inherited to our daily lives.

> For it is **by grace** you have been **saved, through faith**—and this not from yourselves, it is **the gift of God**—not by works, so that no one can boast.
>
> —Ephesians 2:8–9

We are **saved** by **grace** through **faith**!

Saved: The word "saved" in the scripture above is the Greek word *sozo* and means, to save, keep safe and sound, to rescue from danger or destruction from injury or peril, to save a suffering one from perishing, (that is, one suffering from disease, to make well, heal, restore to health) and to preserve one who is in danger of destruction. So with this explanation, we see that in context the word "saved" has a much broader meaning to the more commonly understood biblical term of "born again".

We are saved (forgiven, rescued, healed, delivered, protected and preserved from danger) through what Jesus purchased on the cross. As you spend more time in God's Word, you will discover that there is a whole lot more that Jesus purchased for us! And by God's grace all of this became your inheritance upon salvation.

By grace: Grace is God's unmerited favour towards us. Because of our fallen nature, we don't deserve His goodness, love and mercy. But God has chosen to bless us because of His great love for us. "By grace" means that we don't need to do anything to gain God's love and acceptance or to receive from Him; it is undeserved. Jesus fulfilled all the conditions of the law, which means that it isn't about what we can do, but all about what Jesus has ALREADY done.

Through faith: Unfortunately, more emphasis is put on "our faith" than on God's grace when it comes to walking in His provision for our lives. However, when you understand the extent of God's grace, you will realise that it is not about what you can do nor is it about building your faith for what you need. Why? Because it has nothing to do with your own ability or efforts! It is entirely dependant on what Jesus has done by God's grace! It's a FREE gift from God so that none of us can boast.

If you are "trying your best" to do the Word or to build your faith, then you have the wrong focus. Faith isn't about what you can or cannot do, or what you have or have not done. Faith doesn't earn but simply positions you to receive what has already been done! Faith, therefore, doesn't earn salvation and the fullness of what Jesus did on the cross. But rather, it is through faith in Jesus that you have salvation along with everything else that He has purchased for you.

When we focus on the need to build our faith so that we can receive healing, we bypass Jesus and God's grace. The focus becomes "our faith" and what we can do, and we begin to approach God based on our own performance. I experienced this when I began to have more of a relationship with the literal Word of God than with the Healer—the living Word of God, the author and perfecter of my faith. I was constantly confessing, declaring and trying to get my breakthrough. Consequently, healing didn't manifest because not only was I trying to lay hold of what was already mine, I was also operating in dead works. I was doing everything "I knew" trying to get what I needed. I didn't understand at the time that because I was already saved, I had already received healing. I didn't need to apply a formula; I simply had to apply the truth of what was already mine! Since coming to this revelation, whenever I am challenged, I simply continue to walk by this truth by applying what Jesus has already done and victory soon comes!

Can Our Past Hinder Our Breakthrough?

One area that I haven't yet specifically covered is our past. Remember, we are already saved—by grace—through faith! This means that what you did in your past will not prevent you from receiving your inheritance. It might, however, prevent you from walking in it—if you allow it to. But your past cannot block you from receiving. Why? Because of your faith in Jesus you have already received everything you need for both this life and for the one to come!

I have ministered to many people who didn't feel worthy to receive from God because of what they had done in their past. Unworthiness, guilt and shame are lies that prevent you from having confidence in your relationship with God and from feeling worthy to walk in His blessings. Always remember that what Jesus purchased on the cross for us was a FREE gift. Therefore, it doesn't matter what you have done in the past. You have been forgiven and God remembers your sin no more! In fact, God has told us that He has cast the sins of our past into a "sea of forgetfulness". And there is no longer any need for you to remember them either, because as far as God is concerned, they no longer exist!

How To Walk By Faith

> For we walk by faith, not by sight. [The Amp says...not by sight or appearance].
>
> —2 Corinthians 5:7, nkjv

We are called to walk by faith and not by sight or appearance. This is because our five senses can deceive us. While we live in the world, as believers we are no longer of the world, so we should not live our lives based on the world's standards or on what we see, feel or hear. We are called to live focusing on God's faithfulness and walking by faith, not by sight, feelings or appearances, because not only can these things change, they are also unreliable!

> So we fix our eyes not on what is seen, but on what is unseen. For what is seen is temporary, but what is unseen is eternal.
>
> —2 Corinthians 4:18

To live and walk by faith is to simply live and walk by what Jesus has accomplished on the cross for us, and not by our own efforts or by what the natural circumstances are dictating. This doesn't mean that we deny the facts of our situation or what our senses say to us. It just means that we do not focus on them and allow them to be greater than the truth of who Jesus is, what He has done and what we have already inherited in Him.

Once we have discovered in God's Word the fullness of what Jesus purchased for us, it is our responsibility to then meditate on that truth until revelation and understanding come. In other words, we need to believe what it says. Believing, however, is not based on our natural thinking and understanding because it is not mere mental assent—"agreeing with" God's Word from a purely intellectual standpoint. Instead, believing comes from knowing what the Word is saying to us personally. This will enable us to live and walk by that truth, and not by what the natural realm is dictating. On the other hand, if we don't believe God's Word, and we are challenged with an adverse or opposing situation, then all we have to respond to are our natural circumstances.

What Walking By Faith Is Not

If you have a desire to see the power of God released in your life to change your natural circumstances, you will need to know how to walk by faith (by the finished work of the cross) and not by sight, feelings or appearances. But before I can describe to you the simplicity of what walking by faith is, I believe that it is necessary to first highlight what walking by faith is **not**:

- **Walking by the world's way!**

We need to stop submitting to the world's standards and ways of doing things because the more we listen to the world and submit to its ideals, the more carnal (sense realm) minded we become. If we submit only to this world and to man, then we will always be limited to the natural realm and to what man can do for us. Instead, we need to remind ourselves of our true heritage: We are ambassadors and fellow citizens of the household of God. We are also joint-heirs with Christ and are seated with Him in heavenly places (Romans 8:16, Ephesians 2:6). We should not be strangers to God's kingdom and to His ways because with God nothing is ever impossible. So if we want to see God's power released in our life, then we need to stop listening to, running to and conforming to this world's way and be transformed by renewing our minds with God's way, which is what His Word of truth says (Romans 12:2).

- **Walking by what the natural realm or senses are dictating** (by good or bad feelings or emotions, what we see, the absence or presence of adverse symptoms, or by a doctor's diagnosis).

God's power isn't based upon natural feelings and emotions, either positive or negative. And walking by faith is not based on what we can or cannot see or feel, or what the natural circumstances are dictating, or upon what you can or cannot do by your own natural ability!

I have ministered to many people who have felt positive about their health or situation, but when the doubts or adverse symptoms began, they lost sight of the truth of God's Word and were overcome by the natural circumstances. I have also met those who have placed their confidence in the positive condition of their circumstances. However, just because things look good doesn't mean that everything is going well or that you won't be challenged. Feelings, symptoms and natural circumstances come and go and can change. They aren't necessarily wrong. However, my point is that they are just natural feelings, symptoms or circumstances.

We need to walk by what we know to be the truth in God's Word and not by feelings, symptoms or natural circumstances. We need to train our natural man (mind, will, emotions, feelings and physical body) to line up with what the Word says is fact through the finished work of the cross. It is imperative that we let our spirit man and not the natural man determine what we believe, how we will behave and how we will live out our day.

If we focus on the natural realm, we can build an account in our minds of why the Word cannot work in our lives. This is especially true when we allow our natural circumstances, feelings, diagnosis, symptoms or fears to appear greater or more powerful than what we know God's Word says. When this happens we allow the circumstances to undermine the integrity of the Word and we may not be able to act on the truth when we are challenged. It is therefore important that we don't allow anything in the natural realm to blind us and cause us to lose sight of God's truth and His nature, character, goodness and power.

- **Walking by presumption, hope or wishful thinking.**
- **Walking by mental assent** (to "agree with" what God says in His Word from an intellectual or mental standpoint only). God's kingdom is spiritually discerned, not naturally understood!
- **Walking by works or performance** (what you can or cannot do, or what you have or have not done).
- **Walking by following rules, steps or a formula** (simply following something without revelation is not only powerless but also leads to frustration).
- **Walking by a "name it and claim it" formula** (as if by simply saying something that it will automatically come to pass).

The confession (to agree with or to say the same thing) of our mouth is the out-working of faith (of what we believe in our heart), but declaring, confessing or speaking God's Word is not something we do to make the Word work or to make God do something for us. Instead, we confess, declare and speak out of our mouth what has already been done! We confess what **we have received** because of what Jesus has already established through the finished work of the cross.

- **Walking by prophecies, dreams or "fleeces".**

There are many Christians who seek a word from a prophet, dreams or signs from God in place of the Word of God. When someone tries to test

God's will by looking for a sign, this is often described as "laying out a fleece". Gideon tested God by throwing out a sheepskin (fleece of wool) and asking for a sign because he was not confident in what God had said (see Judges 6). Many Christians today seek this type of sign by "laying out a fleece" to hear from God using Gideon as their example as a legitimate way to get guidance from God.

However, the truth is that a new covenant believer doesn't need to seek out a word through a prophet, a fleece or other signs from God. Hebrews 1:1–2 tells us that in the Old Testament, God used signs and prophets to speak to His people, but under the new covenant, He speaks through Jesus—the living Word of God. We already have God's will for our lives outlined in His Word. What more do we need? If we live our lives based upon a word from a prophet, a sign or a dream and something adverse occurs, then hope can easily be lost because there was no solid foundation for that word, sign or dream to be built upon. These things are meant as an encouragement for the believer to confirm what has already been established in His Word, and accordingly we should not base our confidence or trust in these things alone. While the Holy Spirit may lead a prophet or give you a dream, the Word still exhorts us to test these things by weighing them with the Word!

- **Walking by a blind leap or step into the unknown**.

Are we called to blindly take a step of faith out of our situation? Is "stepping out in faith" biblical? There is much teaching that suggests that faith is simply making the decision to step out of our comfort zones by taking a giant leap or step into the unknown. And if we blindly step out, somehow God will catch us or bring a better outcome to the situation. Many truly believe that they are stepping out in faith when in fact they are only stepping out in their own human strength. Faith isn't a hope in the unknown. Instead, it is resting in who Jesus is and in what He has done.

When I began to study what the Bible said about faith, I found nothing to truly support stepping out or taking a blind leap of faith. There is one passage in Scripture, however, that many Christians incorrectly consider to be a biblical example of "stepping out in faith", and that is the account of Jesus' disciple, Peter, stepping out of the boat and walking on water.

> And Peter answered Him and said, "Lord, if it is You, command me to come to You on the water." So He said, "Come." And when Peter had come down out of the boat, he walked on the water to go to Jesus.
>
> —Matthew 14:28–29, nkjv

Many misinterpret this passage of Scripture by surmising that they just need to "step out of the boat" in order to overcome their situations. But if you look at this passage closely, you will see that Jesus said to Peter, "Come," not "Step out in faith"! Peter was not stepping out in blind faith based on something he felt. Rather he stepped out on Jesus' Word that was revealed and spoken to Him personally. Peter's trust and focus were in who Jesus was in His revealed Word and this enabled him to walk in the supernatural. But when he looked at the natural circumstances, doubt and fear set in, and he lost focus and began to sink! We simply cannot do what Peter did by just picking out this scripture and then stepping out and attempting to walk on water. We would need to have something from God that has been personally revealed and spoken to us for that specific situation.

I have seen many believers make radical decisions based upon personal feelings, their desires or from copying what someone else had successfully done when they hadn't actually heard from God for themselves. Consequently, many have faced bankruptcy, broken relationships, serious life-threatening illnesses and many other disastrous results. Sadly, God ends up getting the blame and more often than not the believer is left shipwrecked in their faith. While all things are possible with God, when it comes to making radical decisions, we need to know that we have really heard from God in the first place so that we can act on what He has called us to do. That way, we can continue to look past the natural hindrances and walk by what we don't see to experience the breakthrough we need.

What Walking By Faith Is

Now that we have seen that walking by faith isn't about walking in the natural realm or by our own natural efforts and abilities, it is time to discover the powerful simplicity of what walking by faith is.

- **Walking by faith has vision.**

Even though faith connects us to what we cannot see, faith is not meant to be blind. Faith has vision, for it knows the end result and sees you with the answer rather than without it. This isn't a case of mind over matter, but rather it is about having knowledge, understanding and revelation of the Word of God. We first get the picture for the answers we need in life through reading the Word. We then need to spend time meditating on it until understanding and revelation come and our thinking changes so that we see ourselves "pregnant" with what the Word is saying. We can then apply that truth to our lives by walking by what it says in spite of what the natural circumstances are saying.

I am so thankful that the Holy Spirit has shown me the simplicity of what walking by faith is and isn't. During the early stages of learning to walk by faith, I found myself at times viewing my situation through my natural eyes and understanding because my situation was medically and naturally impossible. During these times, I would often get a picture in my mind of Sydney Harbour. Where the Sydney Harbour Bridge should have been there was a huge void—the bridge had gone! Every time I thought of my hopeless situation, I would see this picture and myself standing on one side of the Harbour and my breakthrough over on the other side seemingly miles away. Then one day, while I was seeing this image in my mind's eye, I cried out to God for a solution. With this image still in my mind, I suddenly saw something strong and solid come and bridge the two sides of the Harbour. The substance looked like a brand new bridge that appeared stronger and firmer than what was there before, and then I heard the Lord say to me, "Faith is not walking blind because My Word has substance and it bridges the gaps!"

When we face certain situations in life, it may feel like we are standing on the edge of a cliff, staring into a vast chasm with no possible way to get to the other side. But that does not mean that we have to muster up some faith to blindly take a giant leap to get to the other side, or step out in the hope that God will catch us. We simply need to gain a revelation of what God's Word says regarding our situation, because His Word is what bridges the gap! It is what links us from our natural situation to the desired supernatural outcome! His Word shows us what we have already received through our faith in Jesus. And when we walk by this truth, it becomes a firm foundation allowing us to cross over to the other side. We simply put one foot in front of the other taking one step at a time walking out the truth of what the Word says, keeping our trust and focus on God. Isn't that simple?

At first, we will need to be vigilant in the renewal of our minds, and resist all fear and doubts. Fear and doubt position us back on the edge of the cliff looking through natural eyes and understanding. Looking through the eyes of God's Word, however, positions us on the other side! Therefore, we need to be careful that we are not walking in fear, doubt or discouragement, but instead are walking by faith, knowing that we have already received everything we need for life and godliness (2 Peter 1:3) through the finished work of the cross.

- **Walking by faith is a firm foundation.**

While walking by faith goes beyond what we can see, feel or know according to our natural senses, there is actually a strong foundation that has been laid because we are walking by what God has already established in His Word. The Amplified Bible describes faith in Hebrews 11:1 as "the assurance (the confirmation, the title deed) of the things [we] hope for, being the proof of things [we] do not see and the conviction of their reality [**faith perceiving as real fact what is not revealed to the senses**]". Faith perceives as REAL FACT what is not yet seen, or revealed to our five natural senses! What Jesus has purchased for you is real and factual, even though you cannot see it. The KJV of this scripture says,

"Now faith is the **substance** of things hoped for, the **evidence** of things not seen." The dictionary defines "substance" as meaning, that which has actual existence, confidence, firm trust, assurance and a foundation; and "evidence" as, proof, conviction, title deed or receipt.

When you purchase something, you are given a receipt of your payment. That receipt is your proof of ownership. And when you understand the finished work of the cross, the reality is that all the provisions outlined in God's Word were paid for in full by the blood of Jesus. How do we know what Jesus has purchased for us? Through knowledge of God's Word! Therefore, what is outlined in the Word is our evidence, receipt and proof of what we have received through Jesus!

Human hope says "I might receive" whereas when you walk by faith—by what God's Word says, then you will know that "you have received"! It's time then to start applying this truth to your life. So start believing and acting on the truth that you have already received the breakthrough!

- **Walking by faith is a rest!**

> But because of His great love for us, God, who is rich in mercy, made us alive with Christ even when we were dead in transgressions—it is by grace you have been saved. And God **raised us up with Christ and seated us with Him in the heavenly realms** in Christ Jesus, in order that in the coming ages He might show the incomparable riches of His grace, expressed in His kindness to us in Christ Jesus.
>
> —Ephesians 2:4–7

We are seated with Christ in heavenly realms. When Jesus ascended into heaven, HE SAT DOWN! His work is finished, so He is now seated at the right hand of the Father. When we believe (have faith) in Jesus, we receive our salvation and we enter into that seated position of rest. We begin our Christian walk in a seated position, which means it doesn't begin with "do, do, do", but rather "done, done, done"!

Remember, receiving from God is not dependent on works or about following rules, or steps to receive something. It is not about doing or saying the right thing to try to get God's Word to work or to get God to do something for us. We have already seen that what Jesus purchased is freely available to all who believe in Him. Therefore, we must make sure that we are careful that we are not looking to our faith, or the number of times we have prayed or spoken the Word to receive from God. Relying on what we can do is works. If we could earn from God by works—by what we do, then faith would be void (Romans 4:14–16) and Jesus' sacrifice would be in vain. Remember that faith doesn't earn anything; it merely positions us to receive what has already been done!

In order to come to a place of rest in our hearts, we also need to have a revelation and understanding of God's grace. Grace is God's free gift of provision that we cannot earn, because through Jesus everything has already been freely provided.

> For he who has once entered [God's] rest also has ceased from [the weariness and pain] of human labours, just as God rested from those labours peculiarly His own. Let us therefore be zealous and exert ourselves and strive diligently to enter that rest [of God, to know and experience it for ourselves], that no one may fall or perish by the same kind of unbelief and disobedience [into which those in the wilderness fell].
>
> —Hebrews 4:10–11, AMP

The only striving or labouring we need to do is to labour to enter into rest. We are not called to labour or strive for anything else. When we look to the natural circumstances, it is easy to lose sight of the truth and become overwhelmed and default to striving (doing, trying, struggling) to get the breakthrough. For this reason, in times like this, we need to continue to labour to remain in a place of rest. We do this by resting in what Jesus has purchased for us, through the finished work of the cross.

- **Walking by faith is acting on what you believe!**

> Jesus said to him, "If you can believe, **all things are possible** to him who believes."
>
> —Mark 9:23, NKJV

No matter how impossible our situation appears in the natural realm, we need to remind ourselves that an impossible situation for us is an opportunity for God's power! All things are possible to those who believe!

> For **with God** nothing is ever impossible and no word from God shall be without power or impossible of fulfilment.
>
> —Luke 1:37, amp

> Jesus looked at them and said, "With man this is impossible, but not with God; **all things are possible with God**."
>
> —Mark 10:27

Note that these two scriptures say that all things are possible *with* God—not *for* God! We co-operate with God by agreeing with what His Word says (on what we have received) and also acting on it by applying that truth to our daily lives. While God is able to do superabundantly far over and beyond what we can ask, think, dream or imagine, it is according to the power that is **at work within us** (Ephesians 3:20).

> **Do not merely listen to the word**, and so deceive yourselves. **Do what it says**. Anyone who listens to the word but does not do what it says is like a man who looks at his face in a mirror and, after looking at himself, goes away and immediately forgets what he looks like. But the man who looks intently into the perfect law that gives freedom [the gospel of Jesus], and continues to do this, **not forgetting what he has heard**, but **doing it**—he will be blessed in what he does.
>
> —James 1:22–25

Once we have gained the knowledge of what God's Word says, we need to then act on what we believe we have received. James 2:17–21, amp, tells us that faith without actions is inoperative, lifeless and void of power. James 1:22 also tells us that we are to be doers of the Word and not just hearers. In the context of these scriptures, the "actions" or "works" (as some translations state) are corresponding actions that are based on the truth of the Word rather than on the natural facts of the situation. And one way we can do this is by believing what God says in His Word and acting on it by exercising authority over the natural circumstances.

If our actions don't correspond with what we believe then we may not see God's power released in our lives. If one day you say, "I am more than a conqueror," and the next day you say, "Woe is me, you don't know what I am going through," then you will be defeated, because there is no corresponding action to what you believe. If you want to see God's power released to change your natural circumstances, then when you say, "I am more than a conqueror," you also need to act like a conqueror and resist the temptation to submit to how you feel or to what you see because faith acts on what you believe. And this applies to healing, fruitfulness or any area of life.

> "Therefore **whoever hears these sayings** of Mine, **and does them**, I will liken him to a wise man who built his house on the rock: and the rain descended, the floods came, and the winds blew and beat on that house; and it did not fall, for it was founded on the rock. "But everyone **who hears these sayings** of Mine, **and does not do them**, will be like a foolish man who built his house on the sand: and the rain descended, the floods came, and the winds blew and beat on that house; and it fell. And great was its fall."
>
> —Matthew 7:24–27, NKJV

Note that the storm came to both the man who built his house upon the rock and the man who built his house upon the sand. The difference, however, was that the man who had built his house on the rock, who listened to God's Word and put it into practice, was the one whose house was still standing after the storm had passed.

The apostle Paul also spoke of the importance of putting God's Word into practice:

> Whatever you have learned or received or heard from me, or seen in me—**put it into practice**. And the God of peace will be with you.
>
> —Philippians 4:9

I have listed below some ways to help you to put God's Word "into practice" and act on what you believe, especially if you are challenged with an adverse situation. It is not my intention to present them as a formula for you to follow to attain your desired result. To use them this way would be "dead works", that is, using them to earn something or get God to do something [not to be confused with "works" (corresponding actions) as mentioned in the passages in James we looked at earlier]. Rather, they are to help remind you of the truth to see God's power change your natural circumstances!

So what can you do to enable you to put God's Word into practice?

- Make the decision in your heart that God's Word is true and act on that in everything you say and do.
- Walk by faith—by what you have received through the finished work of the cross, not by sight or appearances, meaning to overcome doubt, unbelief, what your natural senses are saying, feelings, emotions, symptoms, and also not to walk by your diagnosis and natural circumstances!
- Meditate on the truth, remembering that you already have everything you need to walk in victory—it is finished; you already have the inheritance.
- Fighting the good fight of faith, meaning to fight or labour to stay in a place of resting in who Jesus is and in what He has already done.
- Exercise your authority over the natural facts (symptoms, diagnosis or circumstances).

There will be times when we will be challenged to let go of what God's Word says because our natural circumstances appear too overwhelming, or the fears, doubts or disappointments can seem to get the better of us. It is in these times where we need to put action to our faith by continuing to stand on God's Word, being determined not to let go of what it says. While these are usually the times when we don't feel like doing anything, we are to resist the fears, doubts and disappointments, and take authority over any symptoms or circumstances that oppose what we are expecting to come to pass. So if you want to see the breakthrough, then you need to stop living by what you see and feel, and continue to "do the Word" by acting on what you believe you have received according to what Jesus purchased through the finished work of the cross.

Walking By Faith Is All About Relationship

Over the last few pages, I have detailed what walking by faith is, and is not. However, above and beyond all these principles, faith is ultimately about having a relationship with our heavenly Father. Faith in Jesus connects us to the Father so we can experience His love and come to know and experience that love practically, personally, and expressly through His blessings (Ephesians 3:17–19, AMP).

The core message of the entire Bible is God's great love for us. He loves us so much that He sent His only Son to die for us so that we can spend eternity with Him. I personally believe that making your main focus a stronger relationship with the Father will be the answer to your breakthrough. When you know who God is, trusting Him will not be an issue.

The Amplified Bible translates the word "faith" in scriptures such as Colossians 1:4, Hebrews 10:22–23 and 2 Timothy 3:15 as the "leaning of the entire human personality on God in absolute trust and confidence in His power, wisdom, and goodness". In other words, faith is committing your entire self to believing and knowing that God is good. This trust, reliance and confidence come through relationship because generally we cannot place our trust in someone we don't know.

Before I became acquainted with who God is, fellowship with Him seemed like a one-way conversation—I was the one doing all the talking! But when I learnt to be still and to be led by His Spirit, I realised that God had been communicating with me all along, I just hadn't learnt how to discern His still small voice. When I learnt how to hear and be led by Him, reading His Word went from being a chore to a delight and every word on the page suddenly came alive and spoke to me personally. Scriptures that had seemed purely informational suddenly transformed into living words of revelation and power. Spending time with the Lord also changed from something that felt ritualistic to being exciting and rewarding, as I learnt to experience His love and goodness. I learnt how to overcome fear, anxiety and depression because in His presence is fullness of joy. I also learnt how to overcome times of boredom or loneliness because He is with me wherever I go and He will never leave me or forsake me. I also have discovered how to lean on Him in times of trouble and how to be led by Him to apply His Word to overcome those challenges. I can truly say that there is nothing that anyone could give me that would add to my life. This is because I have all I need in my relationship with my heavenly Father.

I can testify and teach what God's Word says and I can share how I walked that out and saw it manifest in my life. However, when it comes to a personal relationship with Him, this is something you need to learn to experience for yourself. God ultimately created us for relationship! He is not an impersonal energy or force but rather an all-powerful, all-knowing, ever-present loving Father who longs to pour His love in your heart so that you can come to know and experience that love that will forgive your sins, set you free from all the chains of darkness, prosper your soul, heal your body and make you fruitful in every area of your life!

The Power Of Prayer

SEVEN

"The prayer of a righteous man is powerful and effective" (James 5:16).

When you know how to pray effectively, you will begin to see answers not only in your own life, but also in the lives of those you pray for. Sadly, however, many Christians struggle in the area of prayer so they don't devote much time to it. They consider prayer as something they are obligated to fulfil and perceive it as a burden or chore that takes time, effort and work. When this perception is in place, prayer becomes something we "have" to do rather than something we "want" to do. The truth is that we don't "have" to pray, because prayer isn't a requirement of our salvation. But without prayer, our Christian walk may become lifeless, powerless and ineffective.

When it comes to prayer, it is important to note that it is not something we do in order to get God to do something for us. On the contrary, prayer is all about spending time with God, and building our relationship with Him. When we truly know God and His nature and character through a personal relationship with Him, then believing what He said in His Word and trusting Him come easily. This enables us to believe what He says is true so we can then confidently apply it to our daily lives. I believe that it is essential then for us to spend time getting to know God and allowing Him to reveal Himself to us personally as our Saviour, healer, deliverer, provider, strengthener and protector! This is essentially what prayer is—spending time communing with God so that He can reveal Himself and guide us daily into victory through the affairs of life.

I encourage you to take time out of the busyness of life to commune with God and to begin to grow in prayer. Set a time and find a place so that you will be more likely to keep the appointment. Time spent alone with God is necessary to build your relationship with Him. However, you don't have to commune with Him in this way alone. You can also fellowship and chat with Him throughout your day. The more I learn about prayer, the more I realise that I don't have to pray for hours to have an effective prayer life. Quality is more important than quantity. A five-minute heartfelt prayer based on the Word of God is more effective than praying for hours using complicated methods or principles. Prayer isn't about following a set of rules and regulations. If you pray using a method or formula that you have learnt or memorised, it can become legalistic and ineffective. Simply speak to God from your heart.

God doesn't want us to approach Him in prayer like it's a chore or ritual. Fellowship with God is a blessing. The Book of Psalms tells us that He is present in our praises and that in His presence is fullness of joy! (Psalm 22:3; 16:11, NKJV). When I learnt how to declare what God said in His Word, prayer for most situations went from taking hours to minutes! I was then free to spend time with God for who He was and not for what I needed. I now spend more time in worship and fellowship than I do praying "for" things.

I have also discovered that there are some things we don't need to pray for. For instance, when it comes to what Jesus purchased through the finished work of the cross, we don't need to pray or ask God to do what He has already done. We are heirs, so we don't have to ask for what already belongs to us. We simply need to learn to embrace and enjoy it by taking what we have inherited and applying it to our daily lives.

There are also times where we don't pray but rather use our authority in Christ. For example, when we are faced with fears, doubts or an adverse situation, we need to actively exercise authority over the circumstances. We don't ask God to do it for us because God has already given us His power and authority here on this earth. It is now up to us to exercise it! We have God's very Spirit (His resurrection power) dwelling within us and when we follow His leading, He will show us how to use our authority, walk by faith and obtain the victory we need.

PRAY THE WORD

Sometimes, we may not know what to pray, so we might pray or ask for "God's will" to be done. As previously mentioned, God's will for every area of life has been made clear and known to us through His Word. For this reason, in order for prayer to be effective, we need to learn how to pray scripturally. Don't focus on the problem or give it more attention than necessary, but start with the solution by learning to pray with your Bible open.

In John 15:7, Jesus said, "If you remain in Me and My words remain in you, ask whatever you wish, and it will be given you." When you know who you are in Christ and how to release God's power, you will develop a confidence and boldness when you pray.

> This is the confidence we have in approaching God: that if we ask anything according to His will, He hears us. And if we know that He hears us—whatever we ask—we know that we have what we asked of Him.
>
> —1 JOHN 5:14–15

Always remember that God's will isn't what the doctors say, what your symptoms say or what your circumstances are, but what His Word says. So when we declare what God says in His Word, we then have the answers on our lips because we are praying in agreement with the truth in His Word. John 1:1–2, 14 and Revelation 19:13 both tell us that another name for Jesus is "the Word of God". So when we say what God's Word says then we are declaring the life, power and reality of Jesus into that situation.

> "Is not my word like fire," declares the Lord, "and like a hammer that breaks a rock in pieces?"
>
> —Jeremiah 23:29

Early on in ministry, the Lord taught me the importance of exercising my authority in Christ by declaring the truth of what God said in His Word. Both Julie (my prayer partner) and I had spent months praying for the ministry, but were experiencing limited breakthroughs. I asked the Lord to reveal to us why it was taking so long. The Lord gave me a vision. I saw a huge masonry wall standing in our way. I saw that every time we prayed we were chipping away at the wall. The Lord then showed me how His power was released when I spoke what His Word said out of my mouth. When I spoke the Word, huge chunks were coming out of the wall and it smashed into pieces. From that moment on, we began to say what God said and to this day we continue to see an increase in breakthroughs!

Pray Believing!

All things are possible for those who believe!

> And Jesus answering saith unto them, "Have faith in God. For verily I say unto you, that whosoever shall say unto this mountain, 'Be thou removed, and be thou cast into the sea;' **and shall not doubt** in his heart, **but shall believe** that those things which he saith shall come to pass; he shall have whatsoever he saith. **Therefore I say unto you, what things soever ye desire, when ye pray, believe that ye receive them, and ye shall have them.**"
>
> —Mark 11:22–24, kjv

This passage of Scripture shows us the keys to receiving what we pray or say. It says that if you have faith in God, believe and do not doubt, and speak to the mountains (which is the natural situation or what you are facing), then you will have whatever you say! Jesus did not say that you would get something that resembles what you said. He said that whatever you say, that is what you will get. He also didn't say see, understand or feel like you have received. He said believe that you have received!

If we don't see immediate answers to prayer, we can often make the mistake of giving in to reasoning. Reasoning is a mental reaction that will rob us of God's provision every time. God's kingdom is spiritually discerned, not naturally understood. Therefore, walking by faith goes beyond what we see, feel or know by our natural senses.

Hebrews 11:1 describes faith as the substance of what we hope for and the evidence of what we don't see in the natural—yet. God's Word is His will and shows the fullness of the finished work of the cross and what is contained within our inheritance. We therefore need to walk by faith, which means that we believe and act according to what God's Word says and not by what we can see, feel, hear or perceive by the natural sense realm. This means that when the Word says that by Jesus' stripes we were healed, then that is our evidence and proof! When we walk by faith—by God's Word, we know that we "have received"! So when the fears and doubts come or your natural circumstances press against you, declare the truth of what Jesus has done.

Jesus said, "According to your faith will it be done to you" (Matthew 9:29). Remember, we already have faith! And because of what Jesus did on the cross, we already have our victory in the Spirit. It's time to start walking this out! If we understand this truth, then this will enable us to believe and act as if we have already received the breakthrough in the natural because we have the substance (the reality) and evidence (title deed, proof, receipt) through God's Word!

Be Confident In Your Relationship

> In Him and through faith in Him we may approach God with freedom and confidence.
>
> —Ephesians 3:12

When we come into a relationship with God through Jesus, we become the righteousness of God (2 Corinthians 5:21). All our sins are removed and we are washed, cleansed, sanctified and justified in the name of Jesus and by the Spirit of God (1 Corinthians 6:11).

When we approach God, we are not coming by our own righteousness or by what we have or have not done. We don't come before Him as slaves or servants that need to grovel, plead or beg. No! We come before our heavenly Father with Jesus' righteousness freely given to us as children.

> For we do not have a High Priest who is unable to sympathise with our weaknesses, but we have one who has been tempted in every way, just as we are—yet was without sin. Let us **then approach the throne of grace** with confidence, **so that we may receive mercy and find grace to help us in our time of need.**
>
> —Hebrews 4:15–16

We can therefore be confident when we approach God. Remember that you have God's very Spirit living on the inside of you, so be secure in the fact that you can fellowship with Him wherever you are!

Be Led By The Holy Spirit

> Now to Him who, by (in consequence of) the [action of His] **power that is at work within us**, is able to [carry out His purpose and] do superabundantly, far over and above all that we [dare] ask or think [infinitely beyond our highest prayers, desires, thoughts, hopes, or dreams]—To Him be glory in the church and in Christ Jesus throughout all generations forever and ever. Amen (so be it).
>
> —Ephesians 3:20–21, amp

This passage of Scripture doesn't say that it is according to God, but according to the **power** that is **at work within us**! So while God is able to do superabundantly, far over and above what we are expecting, He can be limited if we don't allow that power to flow. Therefore, we need to learn how to be led by His Spirit so that His power can be released to transform our lives and natural circumstances.

Remember that when you made Jesus Christ the Lord of your life you received an inheritance. That inheritance is everything that is contained within the kingdom of God. This means that you also received the Holy Spirit!

> In Him you also trusted, after you heard the word of truth, the gospel of your salvation; in whom also, having believed, **you were sealed with the Holy Spirit of promise**, who is the guarantee of our inheritance until the redemption of the purchased possession, to the praise of His glory.
>
> —Ephesians 1:13–14, NKJV

The Holy Spirit is the very same resurrection power that raised Jesus from the dead and He dwells in you (Romans 8:11). You are empowered with His power and ability to do what Jesus did while here on the earth and to carry out the will of God for your life and in the lives of others.

> But you will receive power when the Holy Spirit comes on you; and you will be My witnesses in Jerusalem, and in all Judea and Samaria, and to the ends of the earth.
>
> —Acts 1:8

The Holy Spirit is the power of God and also the Helper in your prayer life. The apostle Paul exhorted us to walk by the Spirit, be led by the Spirit and to live by the Spirit (Romans 8:6, 9, 13–14; 1 Corinthians 2:13; Galatians 5:5, 16, 18, 25). But how can we walk by, be led by or live by the Spirit if we don't know who He is?

> But when He, the **Spirit of truth**, comes, **He will guide you into all truth**. He will not speak on His own; He will speak only what He hears, and He will tell you what is yet to come. He will bring glory to Me by taking from what is Mine and making it known to You. All that belongs to the Father is Mine. That is why I said the Spirit will take from what is Mine and make it known to you…
>
> —John 16:13–15

> But the Counsellor, the Holy Spirit, whom the Father will send in My name, will **teach you all things** and **will remind you of everything I have said** to you.
>
> —John 14:26

If you want to know how to walk in victory and the steps to take to get there, then spend the time to get to know the Holy Spirit and how to be led by Him.

Pray In The Spirit

> For if I pray in an [unknown tongue], my spirit (by the Holy Spirit within me) prays...
>
> —1 Corinthians 14:14, amp

> For one who speaks in an [unknown] tongue speaks not to men but to God, for no one understands or catches his meaning, because in the [Holy] Spirit he utters secret truths and hidden things [not obvious to the understanding].
>
> —1 Corinthians 14:2, amp

Praying in the spirit (praying in tongues) is not just something we do whenever we pray. It is also for those times when we don't know what to pray or how to express our feelings in words to God. When we pray in tongues, the Holy Spirit puts into spiritual words exactly what needs to be said or expressed.

> …the Spirit helps us in our weakness. We do not know what we ought to pray for, but the Spirit Himself intercedes for us with groans

> that words cannot express. And He who searches our hearts knows the mind of the Spirit, because the Spirit intercedes for the saints in accordance with God's will. And we know that in all things God works for the good of those who love Him, who have been called according to His purpose.
>
> —Romans 8:26–28

When we pray in tongues, we also build up and strengthen ourselves in the things of God thus causing spiritual growth.

> But you, beloved, **building yourselves up** on your most holy faith, **praying in the Holy Spirit.**
>
> —Jude 1:20, NKJV

> He who speaks in a [strange] tongue **edifies and improves himself**...
>
> —1 Corinthians 14:4, AMP

The more time we spend in communion with the Holy Spirit, the more we develop our spiritual senses. When we spend time with Him, we learn how to be sensitive to the Holy Spirit's voice so that we know when He is giving us the unction to do something or the utterance to speak. He guides us in the ways of God, teaches us about Jesus and leads us into victory! When we know how to hear His voice, then we can act on what He is leading us to do.

Practical Help To Get You Started

When praying for different areas of your life, it is important that you spend time renewing your mind with the truth of what God's Word says regarding what you want to see changed. Remember, when it comes to receiving what Jesus did on the cross, it's not about praying or asking God to do what He has already done. Prayer is more about fellowship with God and spending time learning how to be led by His Spirit. The Holy Spirit will warn you of things to come, guide you into all truth and lead you into victory, as well as help you to overcome any fears or doubts. If you do have any fears or doubts don't ignore them. Instead spend time meditating on the truth of God's Word and transforming the way you think about that situation. You do this by continuing to put God's Word in your heart and mind until you believe what God's Word says, and see it as being your final authority.

Get A Vision

Remember that faith has vision because it both sees and knows the end result. Faith enables you to see the things you desire before you receive them, not through your natural eyes but through the eyes of faith. This means to look through the eyes of God's Word because His Word "paints the picture" of what we want to receive.

Habakkuk 2:2 says to write down the vision and make it plain so that you can run with it! You can begin by writing down what God says in His Word as well as any specifics you want to believe for. Make a decision on what you want (and don't want for that matter) and then write it down!

Many have said to me that they haven't prayed for specifics or made a decision for what they desire because they are "leaving everything in God's hands". The thing is that God is not going to do this for you. He has already made provision for you through Jesus and this is outlined in His Word.

If you need a breakthrough in any area of life, know that you don't have to accept everything that happens to you as "your lot in life". Instead of leaving things to chance, act on what you believe and take authority over the natural circumstances.

Now It Is Up To You!

Grab some blank pieces of paper and jot down your prayer points. Anything you desire, even if it seems trivial, or any fears you have, I encourage you to write them down. You may also want to write down any scriptures that are personal to you, or some declarations in your own words. Remember that this is not about getting God to do something for you or to make the Word work, but rather is all about helping you to:

- Transform your natural thinking and understanding until you see your situation through the eyes of faith (the truth of what God's Word says).
- Walk by faith (by what you have received through the finished work of the cross) and not by sight, the natural realm and senses.
- Overcome doubt, unbelief, natural sight and senses, feelings, emotions, symptoms, your diagnosis and natural circumstances and to rest in what God says instead.
- Act on what you believe by taking authority over your natural circumstances.
- Call those things that are not as though they are (Romans 4:17).

If you are challenged, or you know you need a breakthrough in certain areas, then you will be able to act on what you believe. Above all, don't give up hope, but rest in who Jesus is and what He has done for you and the rest will be history!

Your Position In Christ

EIGHT

"And God said, 'Let Us make man in Our image, after Our likeness: and let them have **dominion** over the fish of the sea, and over the fowl of the air, and over the cattle, and over **all the earth**, and over every creeping thing that creepeth upon the earth.' So God created man in His own image, in the image of God created He him; male and female created He them. And God **blessed them**, and God said unto them, 'Be **fruitful**, and **multiply,** and **replenish** the earth, **and subdue it**: and have **dominion** over the fish of the sea, and over the fowl of the air, and over every living thing that moveth upon the earth'" (Genesis 1:26–28, KJV).

God created man to have dominion and to rule and reign on the earth as well as to be blessed, to be fruitful and to multiply. But while God's original plan was for mankind to rule, reign and have dominion in this world, Adam forfeited this right and handed it to Satan through his sin in the Garden of Eden. This means that God is not ruling the earth right now, but He will one day! He cannot legally and justly move in and take away dominion from the devil. Satan has a legal right because Adam handed it over to him (Luke 4:6). In 1 John 5:19, Amp, it tells us that "the whole world [around us] is under the power of the evil one". Paul, in Ephesians 2:2, nkjv, calls him "the prince of the power of the air", who works in the sons of disobedience (those who are unsaved). In 2 Corinthians 4:4, he tells us that Satan is the god of this world.

But praise God, Jesus paid the price for Adam's transgression and purchased back everything that belongs to us through the work He did on the cross. Jesus was the last Adam who redeemed mankind from everything that the first Adam brought upon us! He DISARMED the world, the flesh and the devil. And He gave us His dominion, power and authority.

While God wants us to freely enjoy what He has already provided through Jesus, we still experience life with all of its ups and downs. We still live in a fallen world and just because we are Christians it does not mean that we will never be challenged. The reality is that we will experience distress and face trials of many kinds. But through Jesus, God has made provision for us to exercise authority over what we face so that we can overcome and walk in victory.

> ...In the world you have tribulation and trials and distress and frustration; **but be of good cheer** [take courage; be confident, certain, undaunted]! For **I have overcome the world**. [I have deprived it of power to harm you and **have conquered it for you**].
>
> —John 16:33, amp

God has provided for **every** area of our lives and He sealed it through the work Jesus did on the cross.

> For whatever is **born of God is victorious over the world**; and this is the victory that conquers the world, **even our faith**. Who is it that is victorious over [that conquers] the world but he who believes

> that Jesus is the Son of God [who adheres to, trusts in, and relies on that fact]?
>
> —1 JOHN 5:4–5, AMP

You don't have to live life the world's way, with its natural limitations. Rather, you can experience the abundant life that Jesus purchased for you.

> Now thanks be to God **who always leads us in triumph in Christ**, and through us diffuses the fragrance of His knowledge in every place.
>
> —2 CORINTHIANS 2:14, NKJV

> But thanks be to God! **He gives us the victory through our Lord Jesus Christ.** Therefore, my dear brothers, stand firm. Let nothing move you…
>
> —1 CORINTHIANS 15:57–58

Knowing you can triumph and have victory in Christ does not mean that you will never be challenged. How can you walk in triumph if there was never anything to overcome or triumph over? This needs to be spelt out, because I have seen many fall into fear and disbelief when they have been challenged in something they were specifically praying about. Sadly, when this happens, many let go of the Word. However, if we know who we are in Christ, then we can exercise our authority to triumph over the circumstances and see that victory become a reality.

In order for us to learn how to walk in victory and exercise our authority, we first need to know and understand the fullness of our authority in Christ, and our position in His kingdom.

KNOW YOUR POSITION IN CHRIST

Did you know that through our belief in Jesus and being joint-heirs with Him, we have the same power and authority on the earth as He had? Unfortunately, many of us don't understand this truth, so we find ourselves waiting and wondering why God isn't doing anything to help us. But the truth is that we have already been given what we need for the victory. All along, we have had the power and authority to overcome what we face. So we have been "putting up with" the things in our lives that we should have been "putting a stop to"!

> And Jesus came and spake unto them, saying, "**All power is given unto Me** in heaven and in earth. **Go ye therefore**, and teach all nations, baptising them in the name of the Father, and of the Son, and of the Holy Ghost: teaching them to observe all things whatsoever I have commanded you: and, lo, I am with you alway, even unto the end of the world. Amen."
>
> —Matthew 28:18–20, kjv

God gave Jesus all His power and authority. And that same power and authority is then transferred to the one who believes in Jesus! When you were "born again", the same Spirit of God that raised Jesus Christ from the dead came to dwell in you. This means that as post-cross, new covenant believers, we have the very Spirit of Jesus living on the inside of us. So wherever we go, we don't go just in His name, we also go in His person!

> But if the Spirit of Him who raised Jesus from the dead **dwells in you**, He who raised Christ from the dead will also give life to your mortal bodies through His Spirit who **dwells** in you.
>
> —Romans 8:11, nkjv

> Little children, you are of God [you belong to Him] and have [already] defeated and overcome them [the agents of the antichrist], because **He who lives in you** is greater (mightier) than he who is in the world.
>
> —1 John 4:4, amp

> For in Christ all the fullness of the Deity lives in bodily form, and **you have been given fullness in Christ**, who is the head over every power and authority.
>
> —Colossians 2:9–10

We have been given Jesus' power, which is far above any power of the devil. All things are under our feet so that we might be the fullness of Jesus here on earth to continue His work.

Know Your Authority

> Behold, **I give unto you power** to tread on serpents and scorpions **and over all the power of the enemy**: and nothing shall by any means hurt you.
>
> —Luke 10:19, KJV

If God said it, He meant it! You have power over all of Satan's power. When Jesus said this, Satan was still fully armed! Jesus had not yet disarmed him on the cross. Yet, the disciples were still able to go out in the authority of Jesus and cast out devils and heal the sick! And how much more for us who live under a new covenant!

How To Exercise Our Authority

When you know who you are in Christ, where you are seated and what belongs to you as a believer, you will understand that "as He [Christ] is, so are we in this world" (1 John 4:17, NKJV). All creation is waiting expectantly, even groaning for the sons of God (that is us) to be revealed (Romans 8:19). It is therefore time for us to stand up in our position in Christ as believers and begin to exercise and move in our authority.

Remember That Satan Has Already Been Defeated!

We must never forget that the battle has already been won and Satan has already been defeated. Stop living under the circumstances or under the diagnosis and start living above them. No matter what you are facing, exercise your authority in Jesus and place the situation under your feet.

> When you were dead in your sins and in the uncircumcision of your sinful nature, God made you alive with Christ. He forgave us all our sins, having cancelled the written code, with its regulations, that was against us and that stood opposed to us; He took it away, nailing it to the cross. And **having disarmed the powers and authorities, He made a public spectacle of them, triumphing over them by the cross.**
>
> —Colossians 2:13–15

Satan has been disarmed! Therefore, the only power Satan has in your life is what you allow him to have.

> ...For this purpose the Son of God was manifested, that he might destroy the works of the devil.
>
> —1 John 3:8, NKJV

> [The Father] **has delivered and drawn us** to Himself **out of the control and the dominion of darkness** and **has transferred** us into the kingdom of the Son of His love, in whom we have our redemption through His blood, [which means] the forgiveness of our sins.
>
> —Colossians 1:13–14, AMP

When you understand who you are in Christ, you will realise that you no longer need to struggle with any spiritual attack because Satan's power and hold over you **have already been broken**.

Resist The Devil And He Will Flee!

> Be well balanced (temperate, sober of mind), be vigilant and cautious **at all times**; for that enemy of yours, the devil, roams around like a lion roaring in fierce hunger, seeking someone to seize upon and devour. **Withstand him**; be firm in faith **against his onset**—rooted, established, strong, immovable, and determined...
>
> —1 Peter 5:8–9, AMP

This scripture doesn't say that the devil is a roaring lion, but rather he is like a roaring lion! Jesus has disarmed and deprived him of power—He has removed Satan's "teeth and claws". We need to recognise and resist the lies and deceits of the devil at the onset. This means that the very second we begin to feel challenged, we are to use our authority in Jesus and resist the situation immediately. We are to resist any sickness, disease, pain, fear, complication or the first sign of symptoms when they occur. When we resist (oppose, withstand and strive) against these things, they will flee!

> Submit yourselves, then, to God. **Resist** the devil, and he will flee from you.
>
> —James 4:7

The word "resist" in the scripture above means to oppose, to strive against and to withstand—not to sit back and be passive. Satan has already been disarmed and defeated, but we must still oppose His lies, deceptions and attempts to keep us from attaining victory over our circumstances.

Stand Your Ground!

As we have seen previously, we are not called to "fight" the devil because he has already been defeated. All we are called to fight is "the good fight of faith" (1 Timothy 6:12, NKJV). Remember that faith is simply believing and resting in Jesus' finished work. We fight the good fight of faith by resting in what Jesus has done! And we discover what Jesus has done through God's Word. Therefore, stand on what God says and not what your situation dictates to you!

God tells us through the apostle Paul to "put on the full armour of God, so that when the day of evil comes, you may be able to **stand your ground**" (Ephesians 6:13). He says that when we have done all that we can, we are to continue to stand! The word "stand" in this scripture means, to endure, to adhere to, to persist, to insist, to hold a course of direction, to continue in force, to sustain or to withstand. We need to continue to stand on what God's Word says by being determined to not let go of it so that we can continue to walk by faith in the finished work of the cross and not be moved by what the natural realm is doing!

BINDING AND LOOSING

While Jesus has given you power and authority here on this earth, if you want to walk in that power and authority, you will need to start using it!

> I tell you the truth, whatever **you bind** on earth will be bound in heaven, and whatever **you loose** on earth will be loosed in heaven.
>
> —MATTHEW 18:18

Jesus said, "I tell you the truth..." and this is one of the truths that will set you free! Whatever you bind will be bound and whatever you loose will be loosed! How? By using your authority in Jesus! You have the authority to bind Satan's power and loose sickness, disease, barrenness, depression, poverty, debt, lack and pain off your life, so that you can experience the healing that belongs to you as a believer.

USE YOUR AUTHORITY IN JESUS!

> And this is His command: to believe in the name of His Son, Jesus Christ, and to love one another as He commanded us.
>
> —1 JOHN 3:23

The first step to becoming a victorious Christian is to believe in Jesus Christ. He came so that we could be set free from the power of sin and death and have eternal life. He also came so that we could live a life of victory and peace, not discouragement and defeat. Through Jesus we have dominion in this world. But that's not all! Through Him we also have the power of God's Word behind us because Jesus and the Word are one (Revelation 19:13 and John 1:1–2, 14). We have the whole corporate structure of the universe backing us up when we exercise our authority in Jesus.

> I tell you the truth, anyone who has faith in Me will do what I have been doing. He will do even greater things than these, because I am going to the Father. And I will do whatever you ask **in My name,**

> so that the Son may bring glory to the Father. You may ask Me for anything **in My name**, and I will do it.
>
> —John 14:12–14

> And these signs will accompany those who believe: **In my name** they will drive out demons; they will speak in new tongues; they will pick up snakes with their hands; and when they drink deadly poison, it will not hurt them at all; they will place their hands on sick people, and they will get well.
>
> —Mark 16:17–18

> …"Lord, even the demons are subject to us in Your name".
>
> —Luke 10:17, NKJV

The definition of the word "name" in the original Greek in the scriptures above is "authority". This means that as believers in Jesus, when we do something in His name, we are doing it in His power, authority and person!

> And being found in appearance as a man, He humbled Himself and became obedient to death—even death on a cross! Therefore God exalted Him to the highest place and gave Him **the name that is above every name**, that **at the name of Jesus** every knee should bow, in heaven and on earth and under the earth, and every tongue confess that Jesus Christ is Lord, to the glory of God the Father.
>
> —Philippians 2:8–11

What are you facing right now in your life? Does it have a name? Exercise authority over it in the power and authority you have in Jesus and it has to bow down and obey. If you tell it to be removed, it will be removed. If you tell it to die at the root, it will die at the root. If you resist it, then it must flee!

So what are you waiting for? You HAVE the authority to bind and loose sickness, disease, barrenness, depression, poverty, debt, lack and pain off your life. We are not trying to get power and authority, because we already have power and authority due to our position in Christ. We are seated with Christ in heavenly places far above all rule and authority, power and dominion, and every title that can be given, not only in the present age but also in the one to come (Ephesians 1:21; 2:6). Therefore, stop living under the circumstances. Instead, put a stop to them. Exercise authority over them and command them to change!

Mirror God's Word—Do And Say What God Says!

Another important way to exercise our authority is to look at who we are in Christ through the mirroring of God's Word.

> Do not merely listen to the word, and so deceive yourselves. Do what it says. Anyone who listens to the word but does not do what it says is like a man who looks at his face in a mirror and, after looking at himself, goes away and immediately forgets what he looks like. But the man who looks intently into the perfect law that gives freedom, and continues to do this, not forgetting what he has heard, but doing it—he will be blessed in what he does.
>
> —James 1:22–25

When we begin to look at ourselves in the mirror of God's Word, (found in the New Testament), we will first see our own reflection. But we need to look beyond ourselves and see who we are in Jesus. Regardless of how we feel about ourselves, we need to believe what God says and put it in our hearts and in our mouths, and mirror what His Word says about us.

Exercise Your Authority—What You Can Say

Below, I have personalised a number of very powerful scripture references that reveal our position and authority in Christ. I encourage you to meditate on them and mirror them by speaking them aloud into your life. Continue in this until their truths are established in your heart and you believe what they say. Then, simply apply the truths to your life by exercising authority over the circumstances when the need arises.

Let the redeemed of the Lord say so! Begin to make the following scriptural confessions over your life!

*The Father **has delivered** and drawn me to Himself **out of the control and dominion of darkness** and **has transferred me** into the kingdom of the Son of His love, in whom I have redemption through His blood, the forgiveness of all my sins.* (Colossians 1:13–14, AMP)

God always causes me to triumph in Christ. (2 Corinthians 2:14, KJV)

God always causes me to have victory in Christ. Therefore, I stand firm and let nothing move me. (1 Corinthians 15:57–58)

When I resist the devil he flees from me. (James 4:7)

I can do all things in Christ who strengthens me. (Philippians 4:13)

I am more than a conqueror. (Romans 8:37)

I have power to tread and trample on snakes and scorpions and over all the power of the enemy, and nothing by any means shall harm me. (Luke 10:19)

Whatever I bind on earth will be bound in heaven; whatever I loose on earth will be loosed in heaven. (Matthew 18:18)

Greater is He who is in me than he who is in the world. (1 John 4:4)

Because I am born of God I overcome the world by faith. (1 John 5:4, John 16:33)

If God is for me, who can be against me? (Romans 8:31)

No weapon formed against me shall prosper. (Isaiah 54:17, NKJV)

> *I don't have a spirit of fear but a spirit of power, of sound mind and of self-control.* (2 Timothy 1:7, NKJV)
>
> *I was a captive but now I am free and I am free indeed!* (Isaiah 42:7; 61:1, John 8:36)

I encourage you from now on to make the decision to say **only what God says** about you! I know that it is easy to lose sight of who you are in Christ and what belongs to you as a believer. But regardless of how you feel, remember that you have **the same authority here on this earth as Jesus had.** Therefore, when you feel yourself begin to lose sight of this truth, stop and remind yourself of your true heritage.

Open Your Mouth

NINE

Once we know our authority and position in Christ and what belongs to us as believers, we need to apply this to our daily lives. We discovered in the previous chapter that the way we exercise authority over any situation we face is by what we say. Now, let us look more closely at the power of our words.

> The tongue has the power of life and death, and those who love it will eat its fruit.
>
> —Proverbs 18:21

There is power in our words! Our words can either create or destroy. If a child is raised hearing words like "you are no good", "you are clumsy" or "you are stupid", these words can affect their self-esteem. Words bring either life or death and over time, children spoken to in this way will become programmed to see themselves in a negative light and will behave accordingly. On the other hand, when you speak positive words of affirmation to children, such as how loved and special they are, you sow words of life into them and they will act and behave on that level. When we speak words of life, we eat the fruit of those life-filled words. When we speak words of death, we eat the fruit of those words as well.

Commanding God?

There is a distinct difference between ordering God around and simply declaring the truth in His Word. Many misunderstand this powerful principle and think that by speaking to their situation, they are being irreverent and demanding things of God. When this thinking is in place a reluctance to exercise authority can develop because it appears insolent or disrespectful.

The truth is that God wants you to walk in what He has already provided for you. Why else would He have given you His power and authority? His power penetrates every realm: the physical, spiritual and emotional, and can bring life, health and restoration to your cells, organs and tissues. If you want to see that same power of God released in your life, you need to act on what you believe. And we put actions to our faith by exercising our authority over our natural circumstances and putting what God has said in His Word in our mouths.

It is important to remember that declaring, confessing or speaking God's Word isn't about trying to get God to do something for us, or to make the Word work. We confess what God says because of **what has already taken place**! The work has already been done, so command it to come into manifestation according to **what Jesus has done** through the finished work of the cross!

This is all about enabling you to:

- Transform your natural thinking and understanding until you see your situation through the eyes of faith (what God's Word says).

- Walk by faith (by faith in the finished work of the cross), not by sight or appearance.
- Replace any fears and doubts you have with the truths in God's Word that set you free.
- Act on what you believe by taking authority over your natural circumstances.
- Call those things that are not as though they were (Romans 4:17).

Putting Your Words Into Action

> ..."Have faith in God. For assuredly, I say to you, **whoever says** to this mountain, 'Be removed and be cast into the sea,' and **does not doubt in his heart**, but **believes** that those things **he says** will be done, he **will have whatever he says.**"
>
> —Mark 11:22–23, NKJV

Note that Mark 11:22–23 mentions the word "says" **three** times.

- "whoever **says** to this mountain"
- "believes that those things he **says** will be done"
- "he will have whatever he **says**"

So what are you saying? Remember, we act on what we believe by taking authority over the natural symptoms, circumstances, fears and doubts by **speaking to them**. The natural symptoms and circumstances will "speak" to you, so you need to exercise authority over them and speak to them instead!

> He [Jesus] replied, "If you have faith as small as a mustard seed, **you can say** to this mulberry tree, 'Be uprooted and planted in the sea,' and it will obey you."
>
> —Luke 17:6

> He [Jesus] replied, "...I tell you the truth, if you have faith as small as a mustard seed, **you can say** to this mountain, 'Move from here to

> there' and it will move. Nothing will be impossible for you."
>
> —Matthew 17:20

Don't speak to God about your mountain, but speak to your mountain about God! Stop speaking about the mountains, situations or circumstances in your life and begin to speak to them. In other words, speaking about your circumstances will change nothing, but speaking to them with your God-given authority will. Put simply, say what God's Word says. If you believe God's Word is true then do what it says. And if something opposing comes, then act on what you believe and exercise your authority over the situation. Declare the truth of what God has done and command the reality of that truth to manifest.

> "No weapon formed against you shall prosper, and every tongue which rises against you in judgement **you shall condemn.** This is the heritage of the servants of the Lord, and their righteousness is from Me," says the Lord.
>
> —Isaiah 54:17, NKJV

It is clear in the scripture above that we are to condemn or refute the tongues (and situations) that rise up in judgment against us. God is not going to exercise His authority for us because it is our responsibility! As we have already seen, we have been given all authority through Jesus, so we can exercise authority over what we face in life to experience the breakthrough we need.

Believe What You Say

> For assuredly, I say to you, whoever says to this mountain, "Be removed and be cast into the sea," **and does not doubt in his heart, but believes** that those things he says will be done, he will have whatever he says. Therefore I say to you, whatever things you ask when you pray, **believe** that you receive them, and you will have them.
>
> —Mark 11:23–24, NKJV

When it comes to saying what God says in His Word, we can't just simply speak out something and expect a result. We need to believe it and not doubt it in our hearts. Additionally, we can't believe one thing and then confess something else because our heart and confession need to work together in agreement.

> It is written: "I believed; therefore I have spoken." With that same spirit of faith we also believe and therefore speak.
>
> —2 Corinthians 4:13

When you have a revelation of the truth of God's Word in your heart, you will automatically speak out what you believe. If you have to keep reminding yourself of your confession and what you believe, then continue to meditate on the Word until revelation comes. Once you believe God's Word, you won't have to keep reminding yourself to speak it out because from the overflow of your heart your mouth will speak.

> ...For **out of the overflow of the heart the mouth speaks**. The good man brings good things out of the good stored up in him, and the evil man brings evil things out of the evil stored up in him.
>
> —Matthew 12:34–35

When you keep God's Word pertaining to your situation in your heart in abundance, the overflow of your words will line up with what you believe in your heart. And once the Word of God releases that faith within, and you declare it out of your mouth, your mountains will be removed!

Positive Words Create Change

I recently read a pamphlet I found in a medical centre on how to manage depression. It spoke about a program where people with different kinds of depression were taught to "play act" and pretend they were well. They were told to speak only positive words when describing their condition or how they were feeling. The pamphlet concluded by stating that when patients followed this advice, they were not only able to manage their depression and reduce their medication, but many of the patients no longer needed medication at all! This included people who had suffered long term and severe types of depression.

This is a great example of the incredible authority we have over our own lives and how that authority is released through the words that we speak. Remember, this pamphlet was using examples of people in the world who had no idea of the power of their words. Yet, they had unwittingly tapped into this powerful God-designed principle. It is such a shame that many people in the world understand and use this principle and reap the results more than many of God's own children!

Dr David (Paul) Yonggi Cho states this in his book, *The Fourth Dimension, The Creative Power Of The Spoken Word:*[1]

> One morning I was eating breakfast with one of Korea's leading micro-surgeons, who was telling me about various medical findings on the operation of the brain. He asked, "Dr Cho, did you know that the speech centre in the brain rules over all the nerves? You ministers really have power, because according to our recent findings in neurology, the speech centre in the brain has total dominion over all the other nerves." (page 67)

If you say or think something like "I am tired" or "I feel sick", your body will respond and react accordingly. If, on the other hand, you say, "I feel great today," or "I have strength for all things through Christ who strengthens me," your body will respond to that instead!

> We all stumble in many ways. If anyone is never at fault in what he says, he is a perfect man, able to keep his whole body in check. When we put bits into the mouths of horses to make them obey us, we can

[1]**Dr Paul Yonggi Cho, (1979), *The Fourth Dimension, The Creative Power Of The Spoken Word,* Bridge-Logos Publishers, Gainsville, Florida 32614 USA. www.bridgelogos.com**

> turn the whole animal. Or take ships as an example. Although they are so large and are driven by strong winds, they are steered by a very small rudder wherever the pilot wants to go. Likewise the tongue is a small part of the body, but it makes great boasts. Consider what a great forest is set on fire by a small spark. The tongue also is a fire, a world of evil among the parts of the body. It corrupts the whole person, sets the whole course of his life on fire, and is itself set on fire by hell. All kinds of animals, birds, reptiles and creatures of the sea are being tamed and have been tamed by man, but no man can tame the tongue. It is a restless evil, full of deadly poison. With the tongue we praise our Lord and Father, and with it we curse men, who have been made in God's likeness. Out of the same mouth come praise and cursing. My brothers, this should not be.
>
> —James 3:2–10

James shows us that the tongue plays a huge role in our lives. In the same way that huge ships have their direction determined by a small rudder, so too our lives have their direction set by our words. James also says that a "perfect man" is a man that has full control of his tongue. Every one of us must therefore learn to take authority over our tongue and hold it in check. Just as a horse is held by a bit, we must control our words and be careful what we say.

Sometimes, we use silly expressions such as "I am sick/scared to death", "you make me sick" or "I nearly died when…" without even realising it. Nothing usually happens when we say these things because we don't really believe it when we say it. But it is important to know that when you say what you believe, things change. This can work both for and against us.

I don't want you to become fearful or dogmatic when it comes to your confession. That is not my intention. We simply need to be careful what we believe in our hearts and what we say out of our mouths. This is particularly so in regards to our health.

A friend of mine who had been diagnosed with arthritis would always say "my arthritis" when describing her condition. I would constantly pick on her words, asking whether she really wanted it to belong to her. Obviously, her answer was always no! I was not trying to be facetious, but rather I wanted her to understand my point, and instead of submitting to the condition, begin to exercise her authority over the condition. Thankfully, we were close friends and she was mature enough in God to see my point and heed my advice. She then started to "talk to" her condition rather than always "talk about" it. She exercised her authority over the diagnosis and symptoms and healing soon took place in her body.

As you can see, if we are giving something a legal right to afflict us through letting it run its course unchallenged, or by calling it our own by saying "my sickness", then it has the right to be there—its existence is reinforced by what we believe and by what we are saying. So stop living under the diagnosis and talking about the symptoms and condition, and instead master your tongue, just like a bit masters a horse, and begin to speak to the condition! Take authority over any sickness, disease, pain, fear, depression, cancer or heart disease, and tell them to be removed. Don't submit to them or own them. Instead, rebuke them!

I want to make it clear that I am not talking about denying the existence of your physical pain, sickness or condition, but rather encouraging you to exercise your God-given authority over your life and possess the healing that God has already provided for you. When you resist the symptoms or circumstances and declare to them what God has done, through your words you are releasing the power to change your situation!

God's Words Have Creative Power

> Through faith we understand that the worlds were framed **by the word of God**, so that things which are seen were not made of things which do appear.
>
> —Hebrews 11:3, KJV

We know from the first chapter of Genesis that God spoke and the world was created. God's power was released through His Words. When He spoke, His Words were full of creative power and framed and fashioned what He directed. And God has not diminished in power! He is so powerful that the whole universe is still being upheld and suspended in space by His Words.

> ...**upholding** and maintaining and guiding and propelling the universe **by His mighty word of power**...
>
> —Hebrews 1:3, amp

> For **the word that God speaks** is **alive** and **full of power** [making it active, operative, energising, and effective]; it is sharper than any two-edged sword, penetrating to the dividing line of the breath of life (soul) and [the immortal] spirit, and of joints and marrow [of the deepest parts of our nature], exposing and sifting and analysing and judging the very thoughts and purposes of the heart. [The niv says... for the word of God is **living** and **active**.]
>
> —Hebrews 4:12, amp

Jesus was God in the flesh and, as we have already seen, He was given all of God's power and authority. He then gave that same power and authority to all who believe in Him. Remember that as God's children, we have the same authority that Jesus has! When you know who you are in Christ, where you are seated and understand your power and authority as a believer, you too can see the power of God released in your life through your words! God's power penetrates every realm: the physical, spiritual and emotional and can bring life, health and restoration to your cells, organs and tissues.

When the doctors told Shaun that we would never have children of our own, we didn't allow this report to be our final report. God said in Exodus 23:25–26 that we would not miscarry or be barren. He also told us in John 17:17 and Hebrews 6:18 that His Word is truth and that it is impossible for Him to lie. So we made God's Word our final authority! While our circumstances were real, we didn't ignore them but we knew that we didn't have to live under them because they could be changed by God's healing power. We continued to declare what God said over our situation knowing that God's Word is true, He does not lie, and that we would not be barren, and the result was four children within four and a half years!

We Can Imitate God

There are two biblical examples that we can follow when it comes to the power of our words. The first example is Jesus and the fig tree.

> Seeing in the distance a fig tree in leaf, He went to find out if it had any fruit. When He reached it, He found nothing but leaves, because it was not the season for figs. Then He said to the tree, "May no one ever eat fruit from you again." And His disciples heard Him say it.
>
> —Mark 11:13–14

> In the morning, as they went along, they saw the fig tree withered from the roots. Peter remembered and said to Jesus, "Rabbi, look! The fig tree You cursed has withered!" "Have faith in God," Jesus answered.
>
> —Mark 11:20–22

Jesus knew and acted on His authority. He spoke to the fig tree and it obeyed him. The life of the tree is in the roots, so even though it looked like nothing happened on the surface, the tree had died instantly at the roots (the life source). It took time for the effect of Jesus' words to spread to the leaves and branches of the tree.

You can expect to walk and operate as Jesus did because that is the authority that He has given to you. So when you speak to a situation, you can expect change and even though you may not see any change on the surface, know that it has died at the root.

The second example is from Romans 4:17, NKJV: "God, who gives life to the dead and calls those things which do not exist as though they did".

We can also imitate God by speaking His Word and calling those things that aren't as though they are. Remember that you can have everything God says you can have because His will for your life is in His Word. Also, remember that everything Jesus purchased for you on the cross is real and exists in the realm of the spirit. So even though you cannot see it in the natural, it still exists in the spiritual. We need to rise up and begin to declare the truth and speak life to the circumstances we are facing today. Begin to call those things that do not exist in the natural as though they did! This is how you see what is real in the spiritual change what is real in the natural!

Say What God Says

As we discovered earlier, "confess" in Greek means, to agree with, not to refuse or deny, to declare openly, speak out freely. So confession is to agree out of our mouths with what God says about us or by saying what He has done through His Son. We also learnt that salvation is the pattern for how we received everything that Jesus purchased for us on the cross.

Let The Redeemed Of The Lord Say So

Now that you know the foundations to transform your life, that God is good, that His Word is powerful and true, that you can strengthen your relationship with God through fellowship and prayer, that you have the same power and authority as Jesus and that you release His power and authority through the words of your mouth, make the decision from this point on to say only what God says! Continue to **put His Word in your heart** by **meditating** on the truth AND agree by confessing **it out of your mouth.** Command those things that are real in the spiritual to come and manifest themselves in the natural!

Seeing
GOD'S POWER
Released In Your Life

Experiencing Healing

TEN

Did you know that we are not meant to constantly battle with sickness, disease or pain? In the beginning, God created all things to be good (Genesis 1:31)! Sickness, disease, pain and death did not exist because God did not create them. So when God created Adam and Eve in the Garden of Eden, they were perfect—fearfully and wonderfully made. God had created them to be blessed, fruitful and healthy. Everything within our body was designed by God to function in full health with no complications of any kind. However, many believe that their bad health is somehow God's will, or is a situation that He has brought about so that He can teach them something. But nothing could be further from the truth! God's Word tells us that we were created to be healthy. So if God was making us sick or withholding healing from us, this would mean that He was working against His own plan, and this simply does not make sense.

It is my intention here to share very simply the powerful truth in God's Word regarding healing, so that you can receive a breakthrough in this area. It is not my intention to condemn or make you feel like a failure if you struggle with sickness. Rather, I want to help you grow in God's Word so that you can learn to walk in victory over all forms of sickness, disease and pain.

More often than not the reason we struggle with sickness or disease is as a result of physical complications in our bodies. But, **praise God, through Jesus there is good news**! When you know who you are in Christ, your position in Him and what you have inherited as a believer (all through the finished work of the cross), you will realise that you no longer have to be subject to your body and what state it is in. You can exercise your authority and walk in the healing that Jesus has purchased for you.

What Happened?

If God created all things to be good and for mankind to be healthy, then what happened? Why is there sickness, disease, pain, poverty and calamity in this world?

> And the Lord God planted a garden eastward in Eden; and there He put the man whom He had formed. And out of the ground made the Lord God to grow every tree that is pleasant to the sight, and good for food; the tree of life also in the midst of the garden, and the tree of **knowledge of good and evil**.
>
> —Genesis 2:8–9, kjv

> And the Lord God took the man, and put him into the garden of Eden to dress it and to keep it. And the Lord God commanded the man, saying, "Of every tree of the garden thou mayest freely eat: But of the tree of the **knowledge** of good and evil, thou shalt not eat of it: for in the day that thou eatest thereof thou shalt surely die."
>
> —Genesis 2:15–17, kjv

Adam was to keep the garden. However, in Genesis 3:6, he stands by while his wife eats the fruit of the forbidden tree, and then he takes the fruit from her and eats it too. Many think that God was withholding something from them by telling them not to eat the fruit of the tree of the "knowledge" of good and evil. However, the truth is that God wanted to protect Adam and Eve!

In Hebrew, the word "knowledge" in Genesis 2:17 means, to know by observing and reflecting (thinking about) and to know by experiencing. The day Adam and Eve ate of the fruit of the tree of the knowledge of good and evil, they **experienced** evil. It became a part of them. The word "evil" in Hebrew means, calamity, adversity, affliction, curses, bad, distress, displeasure, grief, harm, heavy, to hurt, mischief, misery, sadness, sorrow, trouble, vexed, wicked, and wretchedness. Up until that point, they had only known and experienced good. But when they disobeyed God by taking the fruit and eating it, their "eyes were opened" and consequently, they now not only knew evil, they **experienced** it. So God had not been withholding anything good from them, but had actually been protecting them from knowing and experiencing evil!

Notice that in Genesis 2:17, NKJV, it says that "**in the day** that you eat of it you shall surely die". However, Adam and Eve did not die that day, did they? They did not die physically at the moment they ate from the tree, but they did die spiritually. Spiritual death was the consequence of Adam's disobedience and spiritual death brought with it eventual physical death. And as we know, there are many forms of sickness and disease that can also lead to physical death. God never intended His children to suffer from sickness, disease and death. He only ever wanted them to experience His blessings. But sickness, disease and death entered the world through sin. Physical death is an effect or consequence of sin. Adam's spiritual death affected the entire physical or natural world.

Adam and Eve had been given dominion and authority over all the earth (Genesis 1:26). And because God had given Adam a free will, He had to stand by and watch while Adam disobeyed His command and unwittingly handed over his God-given authority to Satan. Through Adam's disobedience sin entered and he made Satan god of this world. The effect of sin in the world meant that the world was now in a fallen state. Since then, every person is born in the likeness of Adam (with a sinful nature) and into a sinful and fallen world (Romans 5:12).

God said to Adam in Genesis 3:17–19 that the ground was now cursed because of what Adam had done. This came into effect the moment Adam transgressed. But God's plan wasn't to leave mankind suffering in this fallen state, so through His goodness and mercy, He set a plan in action to redeem and reconcile us back to Himself. He established covenants for His children so that they would be protected and blessed. And over the course of time, God sent His Son into the fallen world as Saviour to redeem mankind from sin and to reverse their fallen state.

The Finished (Or Complete) Work Of The Cross

As we have already discovered, God has already made the provision for everything we need in this life through the work that Jesus did on the cross, and that includes healing of every sickness and disease. The work Jesus did on that cross was a complete work. In fact, His last words before He drew His final breath were "It is finished" (John 19:30). But what does the "finished work of the cross" actually mean? It means that we don't have to wait for God to perform a miracle, or wait for Him to heal us. We can possess our healing right now.

> Surely He hath borne our **griefs**, and carried our **sorrows**: yet we did esteem Him stricken, smitten of God, and afflicted. But He was wounded for our transgressions; He was bruised for our iniquities: the chastisement of our peace was upon Him; and with His stripes **we are healed**.
>
> —Isaiah 53:4–5, kjv

The word "**griefs**", or *choli* in Hebrew, means, malady, anxiety, calamity, disease, grief or sickness, while the word "**sorrows**", or *makob* in Hebrew, means, anguish, grief, pain (physical), sorrow (emotional), pain (mental). Our English versions of the Bible have all been translated from the original Hebrew in the Old Testament and predominantly from Greek in the New Testament. However, many versions of these English language Bibles do not often correctly translate the words *choli* and *makob* as written in Isaiah 53:4 and mistakenly translate them as "griefs" and "sorrows". Elsewhere in Scripture, however, these exact same words are translated as "infirmities" and "diseases" in verses such as this one in Matthew:

> When evening came, many who were demon-possessed were brought to Him, and He drove out the spirits with a word and healed all the sick. This was to fulfil what was spoken through the prophet Isaiah: **"He took up our infirmities and carried our diseases."** [The KJV says...and bare our **sicknesses.**]
>
> —Matthew 8:16–17

Therefore, Isaiah 53:4–5 should rightly read that Jesus took up **all our sicknesses, diseases and griefs** and **carried all our sorrows and pains away**! He took all forms of sickness, disease, grief, sorrow, distress and pain upon the cross **in our place**! We don't have to **cope** with them. Instead, we can **overcome** them through the work of the cross. Therefore, symptoms of any form of sickness and disease are a lying vanity (that is, empty). They are a lie because Jesus took them away! Therefore, if a symptom of sickness or pain surfaces, make the decision to resist it. Take authority over it and declare the truth and say, "No, by Jesus' stripes I am healed."

The Type Of The Brazen Serpent

To further explain the complete work that Jesus did on the cross, I want to show you a "type" of Jesus under the old covenant. A type is an Old Testament picture of a New Testament truth. It was a picture of what Jesus would accomplish on the cross. The type that I would like to spend some time looking at is that of the brazen (bronze or fiery) serpent seen in the book of Numbers.

> And the people spake against God, and against Moses, "Wherefore have ye brought us up out of Egypt to die in the wilderness? For there is no bread, neither is there any water; and our soul loatheth this light bread. And the Lord sent fiery serpents among the people, and they bit the people; and much people of Israel died. Therefore the people came to Moses, and said, "We have sinned, for we have spoken against the Lord, and against thee; pray unto the Lord, that He take away the serpents from us." And Moses prayed for the people. And the Lord said unto Moses, "Make thee a fiery serpent, and set it upon a pole: and it shall come to pass, that every one that is bitten, when he looketh upon it, shall live." And Moses made a serpent of brass, and put it upon a pole, and it came to pass, that if a serpent had bitten any man, when he beheld the serpent of brass, he lived.
>
> —Numbers 21:5–9, KJV

The children of Israel had been walking in the wilderness and they had begun to mumble, moan and complain, claiming that it would have been better for them if they had stayed in Egypt. In Numbers 21:6, we read that the Lord "sent" many "fiery serpents" among the people and these serpents began to attack and kill the people of Israel. However, Deuteronomy 8:15 tells us that fiery serpents were already in the land and that God had wanted to *lead them through* that place! The snakes were there the whole time that the Israelites were in the wilderness. Up until this point, they had not been harmed as they had been miraculously protected for 38 years. God never intended for them to be bitten. Yet, on this occasion, they were being struck down and overwhelmed by them.

The word "sent" in Numbers 21:6 has often been used as an example of the incorrect theology that God sends sicknesses and diseases and that He kills people who disobey Him. But when we look at the original Hebrew word shâlach, one of the meanings is to leave or let depart. It's interesting to note that Young's *Analytical Concordance To The Bible*[1] and EW

[1]**Robert Young, (1985), *Analytical Concordance To The Bible*, WM B Eerdmans Publishing Co, Grand Rapids, Michigan 49505. www.eerdmans.com**

Bullinger's *Companion Bible*[2] and *Figures Of Speech Used In The Bible*[3] all say that active verbs used in the Old Testament, such as this word "sent" are to be read in a "permissive" and not "causative" sense. Therefore, viewing this passage in this light reveals that God "allowed" the serpents to come, and not "caused" them to come. As a part of His covenant to His children, God had set up protection for the people. But as a result of the curse of the law of sin and death, every time they complained or sinned by breaking His commands, they removed themselves from this protection and were left wide open to experience the effects of the fallen world. God had clearly outlined this in Deuteronomy 30:15–20. They were told to obey and **choose life** so that they and their children would be blessed and would live.

Let's continue with the story.

> Therefore the people came to Moses, and said, "We have sinned, for we have spoken against the Lord, and against thee; pray unto the Lord, that He take away the serpents from us."
>
> —Numbers 21:7

So here we see the people turning to God for a solution to their problem. And **immediately God gave them the solution**.

> And Moses prayed for the people. And the Lord said unto Moses, "Make thee a fiery serpent, and set it upon a pole: and it shall come to pass, that **everyone that is bitten, when he looketh upon it, shall live.**"
>
> —Numbers 21:8

[2]EW Bullinger, (1990), *The Companion Bible: The Authorized Version (KJV)*, Kregel Publications, Grand Rapids, Michigan 49501 USA. www.kregel.com

[3]EW Bullinger, DD, (2003), *Figures Of Speech Used In The Bible: Explained And Illustrated*, Baker Book House, Grand Rapids, Michigan 49516-6287, USA. www.bakerbooks.com

The Lord gave Moses instructions to make a serpent of bronze and set it on a pole so that everyone could look upon it. Those who looked at the bronze serpent lived. The people had asked God to take away the serpents, BUT God told Moses to make one out of bronze and stick it on a pole! God didn't take the serpents away—He deprived them of power! They couldn't hurt the Israelites anymore! The VERY SOURCE of their pain, poison and death was nailed on a pole and DISARMED!

The fiery serpents spoken of in this passage were therefore a type of Satan and his power, and the bronze serpent on the pole was a type of Jesus on the cross!

> And as Moses lifted up the serpent in the wilderness, even so must the Son of Man be lifted up, that whoever believes in Him should not perish but have eternal life.
>
> —John 3:14–15, NKJV

When Jesus took our sins to the cross, He also took Satan and his power over us to the cross (Hebrews 2:14, AMP). Jesus has nailed the devil to the cross for us! Jesus became our sin offering and took our sin in our place!

> And you, being dead in your trespasses and the uncircumcision of your flesh, He has made alive together with Him, having forgiven you all trespasses, having wiped out the handwriting of requirements that was against us, which was contrary to us. And He has taken it out of the way, having nailed it to the cross. Having disarmed principalities and powers, He made a public spectacle of them, triumphing over them in it.
>
> —Colossians 2:13–15, NKJV

> ...that by [going through] death He might bring to nought and make of no effect him who **had** the power of death—that is, the devil.
>
> —Hebrews 2:14, AMP

The very reason Jesus came to live and die was to release us from Satan's grip (to set us free from sin and all the consequences of sin).

> ...and the Lord has laid on Him the iniquity of us all.
>
> —Isaiah 53:6, NKJV

> For He made Him who knew no sin to be sin for us, that we might become the righteousness of God in Him.
>
> —2 Corinthians 5:21, NKJV

> But if we [really] are living and walking in the Light, as He [Himself] is in the Light, we have [true, unbroken] fellowship with one another, and the blood of Jesus Christ His Son cleanses (removes) us **from all sin** and guilt [keeps us **cleansed from sin in all its forms and manifestations**].
>
> —1 John 1:7, AMP

Jesus became the curse for us. Man's sin and its consequences (that is, the curse, including sickness, pain and death—all the result of spiritual death in Adam) were laid upon Jesus. Isaiah 52:14 says that Jesus' appearance was marred (disfigured) more than any other man. Isaiah 53:4–5 shows the punishment Jesus bore. He bore our griefs (sicknesses and diseases) and carried our sorrows (pains) and was wounded and bruised.

> ...He bore [and took away] the sin of many and made intercession for the transgressors (the rebellious).
>
> —Isaiah 53:12, AMP

Jesus Took Sin And The Root Of Sin

Do you see the picture here? Spiritually speaking, Jesus took the poison for us, and became marred and "corrupted to look upon".

In order for the Israelites to live, they must be:

- Healed of their bites.
- Delivered from the fiery serpents (the poison, pain and death rendered powerless)!

> So Moses made a bronze serpent, and put it on a pole; and so it was, if a serpent had bitten **anyone**, when he **looked** at the bronze serpent, he lived. [The KJV says...beheld the serpent of brass.]
>
> —Numbers 21:9, NKJV

Anyone who "looked at" or "beheld" the serpent of bronze lived. For the people to be looking at the serpent on the pole, it meant that they were not looking at the serpents on the ground or at their injuries. The Amplified Bible says that those who looked "attentively, expectantly, with a steady and absorbing gaze" lived. So it was not a quick glance. The word "beheld" (or looked) is the Hebrew word *nabat,* which means, to scan, **look intently at** by implying to regard with pleasure, favour or care; behold, consider, look, regard, have respect, see. When we look intently at what Jesus has done for us, we will experience our healing! And when we **look intently** at God's Word, it shows us what Jesus has done!

Let's have a look at what God's Word says:

> But be doers of the word, and not hearers only, deceiving yourselves. For if anyone is a hearer of the word and not a doer, he is like a man observing his natural face in a mirror; for he observes himself, goes away, and immediately forgets what kind of man he was. But he who looks into **the perfect law of liberty** and continues in it, and is not a forgetful hearer but a doer of the work, this one will be blessed in what he does.
>
> —James 1:22–25, NKJV

> But he who looks carefully into the faultless law, the [law] of liberty, and is faithful to it and perseveres in looking into it, being not a heedless listener who forgets but an active doer [who obeys], he shall be blessed in his doing (his life of obedience).
>
> —James 1:25, AMP

The perfect (or faultless) law of liberty is the gospel of Jesus! If old covenant people could receive healing through faith in a type of Christ on the cross, how much more should we be able to receive healing through faith in Jesus Himself! The people under the old covenant believed in a type (symbol). Under the new covenant, we have the real thing!

As we look attentively, expectantly, with a steady and absorbing gaze at Jesus on the cross, let us perceive ALL of what He has done for us.

He has taken:	Our sins and nailed them to the cross.
	Our sicknesses and diseases and nailed them to the cross.
	Satan and his power over us and nailed them to the cross.
He has provided us with:	Eternal redemption (forgiveness of sins).
	Eternal life.
	Deliverance.
	Healing.

Jesus became a curse for us. Man's sin and its consequences (the curse, including sickness, disease, pain and death—all the result of spiritual death in Adam) were laid upon Jesus (Galatians 3:13). By Jesus' stripes we are healed and made whole.

The Israelites saw the source of their pain and sickness on the pole disarmed and deprived of power, and they were healed and lived. Therefore, I encourage you to see your condition on Jesus' body on the cross also deprived and disarmed of any power to harm you! See any form of sickness, disease, pain and depression on Jesus' body on the cross, deprived and disarmed. Stop looking at the source (your symptoms or diagnosis) and start looking at the solution! Do not look at or behold your natural sickness, disease or pain any longer. Instead, FIX your eyes on Jesus—the author and perfecter of your faith!

The Curse Of The Law

Deuteronomy 28 lists the blessings and curses under the law. Verses 1–13 list all the blessings that came through obedience to the law and verses 15–68 lists the curses that came as a result of disobedience to the law.

As you read verses 1–14, you will find a list of God's blessings of fruitfulness, prosperity, health and protection in every area of life. We have discovered that God only created mankind to be blessed, prosperous and fruitful, and that sickness and disease of every kind came as a result of sin being introduced because of the fall of Adam and Eve in the Garden of Eden. God's plan for mankind did not change. He continued to reveal His true nature and character as healer, deliverer, provider and protector, and we discover this throughout the old covenant. These blessings are listed on the following pages:

Verse	Blessing	What the blessing means
Deuteronomy 28:1–2, AMP	If you will listen diligently to the voice of the Lord your God, being watchful to do all His commandments which I command you this day, the Lord your God will set you high above all the nations of the earth. And all these blessings shall come upon you and **overtake you** if you heed the voice of the Lord your God.	God's plan from the beginning was for His children to be blessed in every area of life. And God not only wanted His blessings to follow them, but also to overtake them so that whatever they put their hand to would be fruitful and bring increase into their lives.

Deuteronomy 28:3, NKJV	Blessed shall you be in the city, and blessed shall you be in the country.	The city here represents the market place, entertainment, justice systems, education, hospitals, transport and communications, media, sporting, industries, finances, banking systems and housing. The country represents the grain crops, dairy produce, animal farms, rivers, rainfall, seed for planting and harvesting.
Deuteronomy 28:4, NKJV	Blessed shall be the fruit of your body, the produce of your ground and the increase of your herds, the increase of your cattle and the offspring of your flocks.	Our wombs will be blessed. We CAN have children and they will be blessed. Even our jobs will be blessed!
Deuteronomy 28:5, NKJV	Blessed shall be your basket and your kneading bowl.	We will be blessed with more than enough! There will be enough food for cooking to satisfy our family.
Deuteronomy 28:6, NKJV	Blessed shall you be when you come in, and blessed shall you be when you go out.	We will be blessed wherever we go!

Deuteronomy 28:7, NKJV	The Lord will cause your enemies who rise against you to be defeated before your face; they shall come out against you one way and flee before you seven ways.	We will have victory over all of our enemies!
Deuteronomy 28:8, NKJV	The Lord will command the blessing on you in your storehouses and in all to which you set your hand, and He will bless you in the land which the Lord your God is giving you.	Our businesses will be successful and prosperous. Our storehouses (our bank accounts) will be blessed!
Deuteronomy 28:9, NKJV	The Lord will establish you as a holy people to Himself, just as He has sworn to you, if you keep the commandments of the Lord your God and walk in His ways.	When we serve and follow the Lord with all our heart, these blessings will come upon us and overtake us! (See also Deuteronomy 28:2.)
Deuteronomy 28:10, NKJV	Then all peoples of the earth shall see that you are called by the name of the Lord, and they shall be afraid of you.	Everyone will see that we are blessed because we belong to God! They will fear us because of our wealth and protection from the Lord.

Deuteronomy 28:11, NKJV	And the Lord will grant you plenty of goods, in the fruit of your body, in the increase of your livestock, and in the produce of your ground, in the land of which the Lord swore to your fathers to give you.	This verse re-affirms verse 4.
Deuteronomy 28:12, NKJV	The Lord will open to you His good treasure, the heavens, to give the rain to your land in its season, and to bless all the work of your hand. You shall lend to many nations, but you shall not borrow.	We will have rain on our crops and seed in season so that we will reap from what we have sown. We will be so blessed financially that we will lend to many but borrow from no one!
Deuteronomy 28:13, NKJV	And the Lord will make you the head and not the tail; you shall be above only, and not be beneath, if you heed the commandments of the Lord your God, which I command you today, and are careful to observe them.	We can live above our circumstances. Whatever happens to us, we will have the ability to rise above it and walk in victory over it!

Moses specifically gave these blessings to the children of Israel, the descendants of Abraham. However, God's blessings were not exclusive to the Israelites, but were intended for all of mankind. His plans are all about increasing—not decreasing. Even under the old covenant, when His children were in exile, His plans were still for them to be healthy, blessed and fruitful. His plans were not to harm them, but to bless them and give them hope and a future (Jeremiah 29:11).

> This is what the Lord Almighty, the God of Israel, says to all those I carried into exile from Jerusalem to Babylon: "Build houses and settle down; plant gardens and eat what they produce. Marry and have sons and daughters; find wives for your sons and give your daughters in marriage, so that they too may have sons and daughters. **Increase in number there; do not decrease.**"
>
> —Jeremiah 29:4–6

And God has not changed! He still delights in His children being blessed, prosperous, healthy and increasing in number!

As I have already revealed earlier, as a new covenant believer, the Old Testament blessings given to Abraham and to his descendants are still relevant to us today. God promised Abraham that all the peoples of the earth would be blessed through him. We know as a new covenant believer that if "you belong to Christ, then you are Abraham's seed, and heirs according to the promise" (Galatians 3:29). Therefore, we are heirs to the very same blessings (Galatians 3:6, 9).

Consider also that if God's plan was different for the new covenant believer, then that would mean that God had changed His mind and will for mankind. But we know that God does not change (Malachi 3:6). He is the same today and He will remain the same forever (Hebrews 13:8). In addition, as believers in Jesus Christ, we have a better covenant based on better promises than those of the old covenant (Hebrews 8:6). In fact, Jesus fulfilled all the promises and blessings in the old covenant, reversed the curse and paid the price for the healing of all sicknesses and diseases. The price **has been paid in full**. Therefore, the same blessings of health, wealth and fruitfulness available to those under the old covenant are available to us today!

Blessed And Healthy By Design—Perfect Health Is God's Blessing

You were not created to be sick, diseased or in pain! If there is something missing in your body, it can be replaced. If something has been damaged, it can be restored, and if there is a sickness or disease, it can be removed! Jesus came so that you may have life and life more abundantly (John 10:10).

> Praise be to the God and Father of our Lord Jesus Christ, **who has blessed** us in the heavenly realms with every spiritual blessing in Christ.
>
> —Ephesians 1:3

God HAS blessed us! Past tense! Some of the spiritual blessings that we have through our salvation in Jesus are forgiveness, deliverance and the Holy Spirit, including the gifts and fruit of the Spirit. We have also been given the same authority as Jesus and we can minister the power of God not only to our own lives but to others as well. We have these spiritual blessings along with all of the blessings of Abraham (as I have just shown)! These blessings are ours through Christ under the new covenant. Unfortunately, many of us aren't experiencing this. So what are you waiting for? It is time to know the truth and apply it to your life by acting on what it says. Once we receive the revelation that we have been blessed by faith in Jesus, we can begin to experience this "blessing of Abraham" and have ALL of the blessings come upon and overtake us (Deuteronomy 28:2)!

The Curses

As we have just discovered, God set up a covenant to bless mankind. God's children could receive forgiveness of sins and receive His protection from the fallen state of the world. However, under the law, the blessings were conditional on the people's obedience. If the people obeyed the Lord, then every aspect of their lives would be blessed. However, just as obedience brought blessings, disobedience would leave them unprotected and open to experience the curses.

> But if you will not obey the voice of the Lord your God, being watchful to do all His commandments and His statutes which I command you this day, then all these curses shall come upon you **and overtake you.**
>
> —Deuteronomy 28:15, AMP

Following Deuteronomy 28:15 is an extensive list of curses, which speaks of destruction in every area of life. These curses meant that the people would suffer from sickness, barrenness and poverty. Their children would also be cursed, together with everything they put their hands to. They would also have no rest from their enemies and all of this would eventually bring total devastation to every area of their lives. The curses are a complete opposite to the blessings. There was no hope for those who were not in relationship with God or who had forsaken His covenant.

God did not create the curses; they were already operating in the fallen world and were introduced through sin. Whenever the children of God failed to keep the law, they broke fellowship with God and left themselves open to experience the curses. It wasn't God cursing them, but rather through their own disobedience, they walked out from God's protection and would experience the curses that were in operation as the result of living in a fallen world. The blessings came through works and obedience to the law. These curses came as a result of disobedience to the law. They were in effect there to warn the Israelites and help turn them from their disobedience. Everything was dependent on them keeping the law.

> See, I set before you today life and prosperity, death and destruction. For I command you today to love the Lord your God, to walk in His ways, and to keep His commands, decrees and laws; then you

> will live and increase, and the Lord your God will bless you in the land you are entering to possess. But if your heart turns away and you are not obedient, and if you are drawn away to bow down to other gods and worship them, I declare to you this day that you will certainly be destroyed. You will not live long in the land you are crossing the Jordan to enter and possess. This day I call heaven and earth as witnesses against you that I have set before you life and death, blessings and curses. **Now choose life**, so that you and your children may live and that you may love the Lord your God, listen to His voice, and hold fast to Him. For the Lord is your life, and He will give you many years in the land He swore to give to your fathers, Abraham, Isaac and Jacob.
>
> —Deuteronomy 30:15–20

The children of God ALWAYS had a choice! God wanted His children to be blessed. His covenant with them was for them to be blessed, prosperous, healthy and fruitful. But through their disobedience, by their own free will and their doubt and unbelief, they refused to trust God. We see many accounts where they doubted God's Word and goodness to them, and mumbled, moaned and complained. This attitude was what left them stranded in the wilderness for 40 years, unable to possess the Promised Land that God had wanted to give them. This was not God's decision or perfect will for them, but was the consequence of their own hardness of heart and disobedience.

Redeemed From The Curse Of The Law

God never intended His children to be cursed. He wanted them to experience the blessings. Mankind was created perfectly healthy. God created all things to be good (Genesis 1:31). But due to the fall, many are now suffering with many different forms of sickness, disease and pain. The enemy has corrupted man's nature and God's perfect plan. So God's blessing of:

- *Provision* was corrupted into *lack*.

- *Prosperity and wealth* were corrupted into *debt and poverty.*
- *Health* was corrupted into *sickness and disease.*
- *Fruitfulness* was corrupted into *barrenness.*

But despite the fact that Satan corrupted God's plan, we are not left defenceless. Through Jesus, the price has been fully paid. Jesus redeemed us from the curse of the law, so that it has no legal hold over us any longer. When Jesus was crucified, He nailed all sin and all of its fruit, such as sickness and disease, to the cross.

Praise the Lord, we are no longer under the law, but are under a new covenant of grace! Jesus went to the cross to deliver us from that curse of the law. He was our substitute. He died in our very place under the curse and was cursed for us. Jesus has redeemed mankind from the curse of the law.

> Christ redeemed us from the curse of the law by becoming a curse for us, for it is written: "Cursed is everyone who is hung on a tree."
>
> —Galatians 3:13

The word "redeemed" in Greek means, payment of a price to recover from the power of another, to ransom, buy off. Christ has redeemed—totally removed and released—us from the curse of the law. He was made a curse for us. Therefore, no curse of the law has any right, legal or illegal, over our lives any longer. This includes everything in the extensive list of curses in Deuteronomy 28:15–68. We are redeemed from every part of this list.

We Are Redeemed From ALL Of This!

Verse	What we are redeemed from
Deuteronomy 28:21–22	Consumption wasting diseases—Infectious diseases, chronic diseases, habitual diseases, tuberculosis. Fever—All fevers and viruses, common colds, deadly tropical fevers, malaria, every fever that can be named. Inflammation—Any inflammation in your physical body, including inflammation of glands, nose, eyes, throat, lungs, nervous system, and allergies. Burning fever—Influenza, flu. The sword—from any physical harm and war (see Psalm 91). Scorching blight—Scorching of heat, crops are protected. Mildew—Jaundice, paleness, cancer. Cancer causes paleness and the eyes to go yellow. We are redeemed from anything that alters the colour of the skin.
Deuteronomy 28:23–26	**Our personal lives**—We have been redeemed from drought, being defeated by the enemy, being filled with fear and being severed from using the authority that God gave His people. We have been redeemed from the control of the elements of the earth.

Deuteronomy 28:27	**Boils of Egypt**—Black leprosy, elephantiasis. **Tumours**—Haemorrhoids, swellings, groin swells. **Scabs**—Festering sores, eczema, scurvy, skin eruptions, welts, rashes, redness, cracked skin, excretions of the skin, allergic reactions, allergies, malignant scabs (skin cancer). **Scurvy**—a deficiency of Vitamin C resulting in weakness, anaemia, spongy bleeding gums, bleeding from mucous membranes, rectal bleeding. **Itch**—All skin diseases, all eruptions, scabs, physical itching.
Deuteronomy 28:28	**Madness**—Insanity, diseases of your mind, Alzheimer's, dementia, losing your mind, becoming senile, short memory, lapse of memory, even mental illness in the family. We have the sound mind of Christ. **Blindness**—Cataracts, any other eye diseases, anything that affects sight, film covering the eyes, glaucoma—you don't have to lose your sight. Abraham's eyes never grew dim in old age, because he walked in what God provided, which was divine health. **Confusion of mind**—Distraction of mind, a fear or panic that controls the mind, imbecility.
Deuteronomy 28:29–34	We have been redeemed. We have the protection of God over our families. We reap a good harvest. We have confidence in prosperity. We can enjoy God's blessings. We cannot be stolen from in our lives. We won't go through periods of grieving. We have a mind that is stable. We never have to be fearful. We can enjoy the blessings of God in our personal lives.

Deuteronomy 28:35	**Legs and knees**—Arthritis, problems in the joints, bones, tendons, ligaments, muscles. Any condition in the legs and knees. **Severe painful boils**—Any other ulcers, sores, skin diseases, boils. **Sole of our foot to the top of our head**—Any sickness and disease that would cover any part of our body, from the top of our heads to the soles of our feet. We are redeemed from **any** sickness and disease that would come upon our bodies!
Deuteronomy 28:59	**Plagues**—extraordinary plagues, serious and prolonged plagues, fearful plagues, or plagues of the seed. **Hereditary diseases**—Asthma, heart attacks, diabetes, etc. **Prolonged sickness**—long drawn out sicknesses such as glandular fever and chronic fatigue syndrome. **Recurring sicknesses** and problems. **Chronic sicknesses** and problems. **Any sickness that may be passed down by your family.** **THE BLOOD OF CHRIST IS THICKER THAN THE BLOOD OF YOUR FAMILY!**
Deuteronomy 28:60	We are redeemed from an endless list of diseases that were brought upon the Egyptians.

Deuteronomy 28:61	We are redeemed from **EVERY** sickness, plague, disease and disaster that is not recorded in the Word of God. We are redeemed from **EVERY** sickness and disease that can be named! We are redeemed from **EVERY** sickness and disease that is not named! Christ has redeemed us from **all forms** of sickness, disease, and plague, including the ones the doctors haven't discovered yet! It does not matter what name it has been given, or if it has not been given a name. We have been set free from all of it. Because we are redeemed from the law, this means that we are also redeemed from all forms of sickness, disease and pain, no matter what shape or form they come in!

We have already seen that God never intended His children to be cursed. He only ever wanted them to experience His blessings. This is why in the new covenant there are no curses, only blessings! For the new covenant believer, no longer is Deuteronomy 28:15–68 a list of curses, but rather a redemptive list of all the sicknesses, diseases, plagues and disasters that we are redeemed from!

It Is ALL The Same To God

Jesus paid the price for our redemption from all forms of sickness and disease! The size or severity of the sickness or disease is only evaluated or graded by our minds and how we see the condition. I encourage you, therefore, to meditate on this truth until you know that whether you are experiencing a simple cold, sore throat, headache, infertility, stomach ulcers or even cancer, ALL have been disarmed through the complete work of the cross.

Continue to meditate on this truth until you see your sickness as God sees it—disarmed and powerless. Don't allow any sickness or disease to have an exalted position in your life anymore. We need to stop being spiritual beggars—going for the crumbs under the table! We are not slaves or servants. We are children! Stop looking at yourself and what you can or can't do. Look to what Jesus HAS DONE! Healing is a free gift that we received upon our salvation. We were saved by grace through faith (Ephesians 2:8–9). God will NOT withhold what He has already provided! Healing is your inheritance so you can now freely enjoy what Jesus has done!

PHYSICAL HEALING IS RECEIVED UPON OUR SALVATION

> ...everyone who calls on the name of the Lord will be **saved**.
>
> —ACTS 2:21

> ..."Believe in the Lord Jesus, and you will be **saved**—you and your household."
>
> —ACTS 16:31

The word "saved" above is the Greek word *sozo* and means, to save, keep safe and sound, to rescue from danger or destruction from injury or peril, to save a suffering one from perishing, (that is, one suffering from disease, to make well, heal, restore to health) and to preserve one who is in danger of destruction. So with this explanation, we see that in context the word "saved" has a much broader meaning to the more commonly understood "born again" sense of the word "salvation". And in the same way that we can be saved from any adverse situation, we are also saved (rescued, healed, delivered, protected and preserved from danger) in every area of our lives.

Let's look at some more examples of this word *sozo* in the Gospels.

Matthew 9:20–22, NKJV, recounts the story of the woman with the flow of blood (a physical problem) being healed. In verse 22, Jesus says to her, "Be of good cheer, daughter; your faith has made you **well** [*sozo*]."

In Mark 6:56, NKJV, it says, "Wherever He [Jesus] entered, into villages, cities, or the country, they laid the **sick** in the marketplaces, and begged Him that they might just touch the hem of His garment. And as many as touched Him were made **well** [*sozo*]."

Again, in Mark 10:46–52, NKJV, the account of Bartimaeus receiving his sight, verse 52 says, "Then Jesus said to him, 'Go your way; your faith has made you **well** [*sozo*].' And immediately he received his sight and followed Jesus on the road."

In Luke 17:12–19, NKJV, we have the account of 10 lepers being healed. One returned to thank Jesus, and Jesus said to him, "Arise, go your way; your faith has made you **well** [*sozo*]."

Notice that in every one of these scriptures, it was a physical sickness that was healed. Our English definition of the word "salvation" does not do God's meaning of the word "salvation" or *sozo* justice. Salvation in the mind of God covers or provides for every part of our being or every part of our lives (not just for our spirit).

> And the very God of peace sanctify you **wholly**; and I pray God your whole spirit and soul and body be preserved blameless unto the coming of our Lord Jesus Christ.
>
> —1 Thessalonians 5:23, KJV

We are spirit, soul and body. Only the Word of God can separate or distinguish between each part.

> For the word of God…piercing even to the division of soul and spirit, and of joints and marrow [body]…
>
> —Hebrews 4:12, NKJV

When we received salvation, God provided something for our entire being. Let's take a look at the "benefits" of our salvation.

> Praise the Lord, O my soul, **and forget not all His benefits**—who forgives all your sins and heals **all** your diseases, who redeems your life from the pit and crowns you with love and compassion, who satisfies your desires with good things so that your youth is renewed like the eagle's. [Verse 5 in the Amp says...Who satisfies your mouth (your necessity and **desire at your personal age and situation**) with good so that your youth, renewed, is like the eagle's (strong, overcoming, soaring)!]
>
> —Psalm 103:2–5

God has healed all sicknesses and diseases! His will is for all to be healed in the same way that it is His will for all to receive salvation. However, just like salvation is not always received, it is the same with healing. If you need healing in your body, then know that Jesus has already borne your sicknesses and carried your diseases at the same time and in the same manner that He bore your sins. If you are "saved" by having received Jesus as Lord and Saviour, then you are healed also! Healing is your inheritance upon salvation through the finished work of the cross!

Practical Application

Now that you know the provision in God's Word for your health, you will need to meditate on this truth until His Word becomes your final authority regardless of any negative diagnosis or physical condition in your body. Know that you don't have to live "under" any condition or natural symptom! You have been given everything you need in life through Christ so you can exercise authority and walk in your inheritance of health and healing.

When I first learnt how to walk in healing, the Lord revealed to me that the size or severity of any condition is not an issue because Jesus paid the price for the healing of all sicknesses and diseases. So it didn't matter if I was facing a sore throat, infertility or something I considered to be more serious. The size of the condition was only in my natural mind and understanding. By judging the possibility of healing based on the severity of my husband, Shaun's sterile condition, I was exalting the condition to a place greater than the power of God and His Word. Instead, I needed to bring how I saw the condition into submission to the truth of the Word, which said that "by Jesus' stripes Shaun was healed" and that "I would not miscarry or be barren" (Isaiah 53:4–5, Exodus 23:25–26).

I needed to renew my mind until these truths in God's Word found place in my heart and I believed that I would have my own biological children. And praise God the end result was four children within four and a half years.

Healing FAQs (Frequently Asked Questions)

ELEVEN

We have just discovered that God has created us to be healthy and that He has already provided everything we need through the finished work of the cross. Therefore, if we are faced with any form of sickness or disease, we can apply this truth to see and experience our breakthroughs. However, for some, it can be a process to learn how to walk this truth out in their daily lives. It can take time to overcome wrong thinking, break strongholds of any negative diagnosis or bad report, and renew your mind with the truth in God's Word. In the same way that it takes time for a seed to grow after being planted, to develop roots and grow into a mature fruit-bearing plant, God's Word needs to take root in your heart and go from information to revelation, and become personal to you.

When it comes to teaching on how to see healing manifest, I have found that there are many questions that arise. I feel that it is necessary to come to a place where you are fully persuaded of the truth, otherwise when the questions or doubts come they can cause you to stumble and become double-minded. While I won't be able to answer every question you may have, I would like to cover just some of the most frequently asked questions that I receive so that I can help dispel any fears or misconceptions you may have on receiving and maintaining healing. Let the truth in God's Word set you free!

Question 1: *Does sickness, disease or pain come from God?*

> Every **good and perfect** gift is from above, coming down from the Father of the heavenly lights, **who does not change** like shifting shadows.
>
> —James 1:17

As we have already discovered throughout this book, God is good—all the time! Sickness, disease or pain of any kind are not good gifts, and they never will be! The nature and character of God is always to heal, deliver, set free, rescue and to protect. When you understand His true nature and character, you will understand that:

- Healing is not something that God does—Healing is who He is. (*Jehovah Rapha,* our healer.)
- Deliverance is not something that God does—Deliverance is who He is. (*Jehovah Nissi* our banner of victory.)
- Provision is not something that God does—Provision is who He is. (*Jehovah Jireh,* our provider.)
- Protection is not something that God does—Protection is who He is (Psalm 91). (*Jehovah Rohi,* the shepherd who "shields" the sheep—Psalm 23:1, AMP)
- Salvation is not something that God does—Salvation is who He is!

To be confident in the truth of who God is, you need only to look at His

Son Jesus. Jesus came as God in the flesh. He revealed that the nature and character of God is only ever good. He showed that good cannot come out of evil, and evil cannot come out of good.

> Out of the same mouth come praise and cursing. My brothers, this should not be. Can both fresh water and salt water flow from the same spring? My brothers, can a fig tree bear olives, or a grapevine bear figs? Neither can a salt spring produce fresh water.
>
> —James 3:10–12

> ...every good tree bears good fruit, but a bad tree bears bad fruit. **A good tree cannot bear bad fruit**, nor can a bad tree bear good fruit.
>
> —Matthew 7:17–18

If God is the one who has redeemed you from sickness and disease, then He cannot be the one that put them there in the first place, can He? No! Because:

- Good cannot come off the same tree as evil.
- Sickness cannot come off the same tree as healing!
- Barrenness cannot come off the same tree as fruitfulness!
- Lack, debt and poverty cannot come off the same tree as provision, prosperity and abundance!

If God is the one setting you free, He cannot also be the one that bound you in the first place. He cannot do both because He cannot work against Himself! A kingdom that is divided against itself will not stand!

> Then was brought unto him one possessed with a devil, blind, and dumb: and He healed him, insomuch that the blind and dumb both spake and saw. And all the people were amazed, and said, "Is not this the son of David?" But when the Pharisees heard it, they said, "This fellow doth not cast out devils, but by Beelzebub the prince of the devils." And Jesus knew their thoughts, and said unto them, "**Every kingdom divided against itself** is brought to desolation; and every

> city or house divided against itself **shall not stand**: And **if Satan cast out Satan, he is divided against himself**; how shall then his kingdom stand? And if I by Beelzebub cast out devils, by whom do your children cast them out? Therefore they shall be your judges. But if I cast out devils by the Spirit of God, then the kingdom of God is come unto you."
>
> —Matthew 12:22–28, kjv

Note that verse 26 says that if Satan drives out Satan, he is divided against himself. In other words, Jesus was saying that the sickness came from Satan and if Jesus was working under Satan's power, then He would be working against Himself. If God is putting sickness on people and Jesus (sent from the Father) is then healing the sickness, then they would both be working against each other. A house divided cannot stand! Many Christians actually believe that God is the one who puts sickness on people. But as you look at the above scriptures this is not so! God is not the author of sickness. He is not into afflicting people with sicknesses or diseases. He is light, and in Him is no darkness at all (1 John 1:5).

As I mentioned earlier, to see God at work, we only need to look at Jesus (John 14:7). Jesus was God on the earth. He was the exact image and representation of the Father (Hebrews 1:3). Jesus clearly showed us that the works He did were the works of the Father. He sent Jesus to do good on this earth. In fact, Acts 10:38, nkjv, tells us that Jesus "went about doing good and **healing all who were oppressed by the devil**, for God was with Him". Jesus never gave someone a sickness or disease. He touched people, healed them and removed their diseases.

Often, when people get sick, or die, God ends up getting the blame. But God created all things to be good.

> The thief does not come except to steal, and to kill, and to destroy. I have come that they may have life, and that they may have it more abundantly.
>
> —John 10:10, nkjv

In the Old Testament, God's people didn't know that the adversary, the devil, was the one behind all their troubles. They wrongly believed that everything good came from God, and everything bad came from God. Unfortunately, many Christians today also believe the same thing. However, Jesus revealed the truth that God is the healer and that Satan was the one behind all the sicknesses, diseases and deaths:

- Satan went forth and smote Job with sore boils (Job 2:7, KJV).
- Satan had bound the woman who had a spirit of infirmity (Luke 13:11–16).

The whole purpose of Jesus coming to earth was to destroy the works of the devil, not to enforce or use them. Jesus became sin for us and through the work He did on the cross, He disarmed and defeated Satan and all his works (Colossian 2:14–15). Jesus gave us back our authority over the earth and over the devil that was taken from Adam during the fall in the Garden of Eden:

- Jesus gave us the authority to trample on serpents and scorpions, and over all the power of the enemy, and nothing shall by any means hurt us (Luke 10:19, NKJV).
- The reason the Son of God appeared was to destroy the devil's work (1 John 3:8).

God doesn't want His children to suffer from any form of Satan's oppression. He wants us to walk in our authority and position in Christ, and walk in victory over the devil and all his works. So we don't have to be captive to Satan's works any longer. We can resist them and watch them flee from our lives.

The devil is the source BUT God has the answer! He sent Jesus! He sent forth His Word and healed you (Psalm 107). STOP looking at your diagnosis, symptoms or past experiences and GO TO THE SOLUTION! Fix your eyes on Jesus, the author and perfecter of your faith.

Question 2: *Does God use sickness to test us?*

One of the most distressing things I can ever hear a person who is going through trials or sickness say is that they believe God is making them sick to teach them something, or to force them to come closer to Him. If you believe that God is using sicknesses or diseases to teach you something or use it in some way, then you will not be able to accept that God wants you well or that He has provided a way for you to be healed.

God does not put sicknesses or diseases on people. He is the one who **has redeemed** you from it. If you act as if God put it there, you will remain captive under that condition. It is time therefore to react against sickness. It is under the curse of the law, and Christ has totally redeemed you from every part of this curse. To say that God is the one testing people today with sickness is the same as saying that He is also the one tempting them with sin and this is not truth.

Firstly, God is never tempted with evil, nor will He enforce evil. It is simply not in His nature.

> When tempted, no one should say, "God is tempting me." For God cannot be tempted by evil, nor does He tempt anyone.
>
> —James 1:13

Only good and perfect things come from God. That which is not good and not perfect is not from God. So when people are sick, it is not because God is testing them with that sickness.

In order to begin to see your healing manifest you must know that it is God's will for you to be healed. God says in Hosea 4:6 that "My people are destroyed from lack of knowledge". Many Christians are suffering because they simply lack knowledge of what God has provided for them. This knowledge is found within His Word because that is where God has provided His written will for our lives. Therefore, His will for your situation isn't what the doctors say, what your circumstances say, what your past history is, but what His Word says! So get to know what the

Word says is available to you and then begin to walk by faith by applying that truth to your life!

Question 3: *Does God delay Healing for our spiritual growth?*

Absolutely not! God will **never** withhold healing! If we say that God wants us to wait for healing for some reason then what we are actually saying is that God is withholding the healing blood of Jesus from us! See how absurd that sounds? We have already seen that healing and salvation were provided at the same time and in the same manner. So in the same way that God would not withhold salvation, He will also not withhold healing. In fact, He cannot withhold what He has already given to us!

Unfortunately, many don't know this truth. They wrongly believe that God wants them to wait in order to do a work in them. They use scriptures about trials and tests out of context and removed from their original meaning to try and rationalise their situation by saying that God is using it to make them grow or to teach them something.

> ...now for a little while you may be distressed by trials and suffer temptations, so that [the genuineness] of your faith may be tested, [your faith] which is infinitely more precious than the perishable gold which is tested and purified by fire. [This proving of your faith is intended] to redound to [your] praise and glory and honor when Jesus Christ (the Messiah, the Anointed One) is revealed.
>
> —1 PETER 1:6–7, AMP

Jesus said that we will face trials and distresses of many kinds in this world.

> ...In the world you have tribulation and trials and distress and frustration; but be of good cheer [take courage; be confident, certain, undaunted]! For **I have overcome the world. [I have deprived it of power to harm you and have conquered it for you.]**
>
> —JOHN 16:33, AMP

But look at what else He said: "Be of good cheer...For I have **overcome** the world...**for you**"! The tests and trials that the disciples and believers faced in the Bible were caused by persecution for spreading the gospel, not sickness or disease. It was their faith in Christ that was tested.

All forms of sickness and disease are the corruption of Satan! Jesus has already purchased your healing, so why would God withhold it from you? Knowing this then, don't allow Satan to enforce something in your body that Jesus died to free you from any longer.

Often, when many reach a desperate situation, they decide to call upon God to respond to their needs or to help them cope. God's nature is to work everything for good from things that Satan intended for harm. That is why many people find God through suffering. But they could have grown and been touched just as powerfully without being in a desperate situation.

We need to keep to the new covenant and get to KNOW what Jesus did on the cross. He paid the price for the healing of all sicknesses and diseases. When you asked Him to be Lord of your life, you were born again by the Spirit of God. Your inheritance is NOW from Him. You are joint-heirs with Christ. Does He have any sickness or disease? No! Therefore allow, Jesus' life, blood, healing and resurrection power to flow in your body!

> I am crucified with Christ: nevertheless I live; yet not I, but Christ liveth in me: and the life which I now live in the flesh I live by the faith of the Son of God, who loved me, and gave Himself for me.
>
> —Galatians 2:20, KJV

Jesus has redeemed us. He has reversed the curse! It has already been done! It is by faith in Jesus Christ that we receive the fullness of what He purchased for us through the work of the cross. We need to remember that upon salvation all the inheritance of the flesh and the fruit of sin were put to death (or put to the cross)! Therefore, we need to stop living by the flesh and live by the Spirit of life and the truth of who we are in Christ, and what we have inherited as believers. We are redeemed from the fruit and outworking of sin, which includes all sicknesses and diseases. So why allow what Jesus died to set you free from to stay on your body any longer?

Question 4: *Is it ever God's will for us to be sick?*

> Worship the Lord your God, and His blessing will be on your food and water. I will take away sickness from among you, and none will miscarry or be barren in your land. I will give you a full life span.
>
> —EXODUS 23:25–26

This scripture is a specific promise regarding our health, fertility and lifespan. Yet, many still wrongly believe that in certain situations, it is God's will that a person isn't healed or that he dies.

We need to understand the goodness of God, His unchanging nature and His faithfulness to His Word.

> Every good and perfect gift is from above, coming down from the Father of the heavenly lights, **who does not change** like shifting shadows.
>
> —JAMES 1:17

> "For I know the plans I have for you," declares the Lord, "plans to prosper you and **not to harm you**, plans to give you hope and a future."
>
> —JEREMIAH 29:11

Only good gifts come from God. Sickness or disease for any reason are not good gifts. Romans 11:29 tells us that the gifts of God are "irrevocable". This doesn't just apply to spiritual gifts but to all of God's gifts, including His gift of abundant life that Jesus died to give to us. God created all things to be good, perfect, healthy and fruitful.

Sickness, disease or pain often occurs due to a complication with our health or in our body, not because of the will of God. God created mankind to be healthy. This was His original plan. It was as a result of the fall of Adam and Eve that sickness and disease entered the world and can now manifest in our lives. However, God's nature or character has not changed, even though we live in a fallen world. His Word and character always remain the same (Malachi 3:6). He will never cause us to be sick or to die prematurely.

We need to understand that we can't use our personal experiences to measure God's Word. By this I mean that just because we experienced (or didn't experience) something doesn't mean that the situation was from God or that it was His will. The Bible tells us that God will not alter His promises.

> God is not a man, that He should lie, nor a son of man, that He should change His mind. Does He speak and then not act? Does He promise and not fulfil?
>
> —Numbers 23:19

If we say that it is God's will that we are sick, we are accusing Him of withholding the healing blood of Jesus from us. But as we have discovered throughout this book, healing is already our provision. So **God cannot withhold what He has already provided** through His Son.

There are many reasons and many circumstances that hinder us from walking in healing, or experiencing a miracle, but they are not because God decided to break His Word. God has bound Himself to His Word. He wants you to walk in the fullness of what Jesus has purchased for you. He has also already revealed His will on this issue. You will find it in His written Word, and within it you will discover the provision for prosperity and blessings of health.

God has already made provision for healing of any form of sickness, disease, pain and the causes of these. I have ministered to many people who have been healed, even when all odds were stacked against them. Many doctors have scratched their heads in amazement.

If you are faced with fears or symptoms of a sickness or disease, then don't accept them as God's will, submit to what is happening and wait for the natural course of events to take place. At those times, you need to make a stand and declare what belongs to you. Instead of dwelling on the problem, focus on the solution! Focus on God and His healing power and remind yourself of who you are in Christ. Remember what Jesus said: "… if you have faith as small as a mustard seed, you can say to this mountain, 'Move from here to there' and it will move. Nothing will be impossible for you." (Matthew 17:20)

Don't talk **about** your mountain to God, but talk **to** your mountain about what God has done! So open your mouth and exercise your God-given authority over your body and the natural circumstances. Continue to walk by faith (by the finished work of the cross) and not by sight, feelings or appearances (Mark 11:20–24).

Question 5: *What about God's timing?*

I have heard many say that God is waiting until they are ready, or until they have grown or learnt something, before He will heal them. Let me tell you, this is definitely not scriptural. A lot of people find God through sickness or disease, but that doesn't mean that God caused or used it. In fact, He will work in spite of it. What Satan intended to harm and destroy, the Lord will take and work for good.

Often, when faced with a desperate situation, people call upon God as a kind of last resort. But we don't have to wait until we are desperate to seek God. We can find Him anytime. We should seek Him for who He is and for a deeper relationship with Him, not just turn to Him when we face an adverse situation.

So does God's timing play a part when it comes to healing? Do we need to sit and wait until God is ready to heal or bless us?

When it comes to the finished work of the cross and what Jesus purchased for us, I personally don't believe in "God's timing". This is because it would mean that you would be waiting for God to do what He has already done!

We know that when God created Adam and Eve, He created them healthy. He **blessed them** and told them to go forth and multiply. Adam and Eve did not suffer with sickness or disease. **He made us healthy**! Remember, we don't have to come and ask God for what **He has already** provided for us. If you are struggling in this area, you need to understand that it is NOT GOD WITHHOLDING FROM YOU. God is not making you sick, or preventing you from receiving healing!

As we have already discovered, when Adam and Eve ate of the tree of the "knowledge" of good and evil in the Garden of Eden, their eyes were opened and they knew evil. "Knowledge" means to know by observing, calculating and **experiencing**. Up until that point, they only knew good. We know that the result of the fall in the Garden meant that the world was now in a fallen state (it was now cursed for Adam's sake, meaning as a result of what Adam had done). Satan was also made god of this world.

God's Solution

We have seen that God never changes, so all the blessings of health, provision and fruitfulness provided by God to the Israelites also belong to us as well. They are still God's will, plan and purpose for mankind! So even though the children of Israel under the law lived in a fallen world, God made His purpose very clear that for them to be blessed, healthy and prosperous was still His plan, and purpose.

We Have A Better Covenant!

One thing we need to remember: The people approached God differently under the old covenant because they were under the law (working to earn righteousness). As new covenant believers, we shouldn't be looking to how those under the old covenant responded or how they came to God. The old has gone! Under the old covenant, they were slaves or servants. But under the new covenant we are **children**—joint heirs with Christ—seated in heavenly places **with Him**!

When Jesus died on the cross, He paid the price for EVERYTHING that came into the world as the result of sin and the fall. Satan is still roaming the earth as the god of this world (for a time) and the consequences of the fall are still at work, and this is why sickness and disease are still operating on the earth. But, praise God, through the work of the cross, JESUS DISARMED THEM ALL! He deprived them of power to harm us! He bore them ALL on His body, and He became our substitute. So ANYONE who looks to the cross LIVES! We do not have to continue to be bitten by this fallen world and the effects of the curse of the law. If we partake of the work of the cross, we can overcome and learn how to walk in victory over what we may experience! Isn't that exciting?

Through Jesus, God has made the provision for our healing. And this includes everything that can cause or contribute to any form of sickness, disease or pain in your body.

We know that when Jesus ascended to heaven, He SAT DOWN! His work was complete! We don't need to pray and ask God for what He has already provided because it is FINISHED! This means that sickness and disease and everything that causes them are FINISHED!

Healing is God's plan, purpose and will for all of mankind. That never changes. The causes of sickness, disease and pain are many and varied, but remember, Jesus has already paid the price for ANYTHING and EVERYTHING holding us back from receiving healing and walking in perfect health! So you can clearly see that God's timing has nothing whatsoever to do with healing. Jesus is sitting at the right hand of the Father—WAITING FOR YOU—to go and possess EVERYTHING He died to give to you!

- He gave you His Word (He sent forth His Word and healed you), where you find knowledge, on who you are in Christ and what you have already inherited as a believer.
- He disarmed the devil.
- He disarmed all sicknesses and diseases.
- He gave you His power and authority (so you can exercise that

authority over anything preventing your victory).

- He gave you power over all the power of the enemy (Luke 10:19).
- He poured His Spirit in you (His indwelling resurrection life and power—Acts 1:8, Romans 8:11).
- His Spirit will also comfort you, strengthen you, guide you into all truth, warn you of things to come and lead you into victory!

What more do you need?

If you are waiting for God to do something, you will be waiting a very long time. I meet people who have been waiting for God to heal them. When they finally lay hold of this truth and apply the finished work of the cross in every area of their lives, sickness is broken!

So what are you waiting for? GO FORTH AND WALK IN HEALTH!

Question 6: *What about genetic or hereditary sicknesses and diseases?*

As we have already discovered, Jesus has redeemed us from the curse of the law and all forms of sickness and disease, including the inherited ones!

God's design for the human race was for us to be healthy. Unfortunately, many can experience sickness because the world is fallen.

When it comes to the issue of hereditary and genetic sicknesses and diseases, I thank God that the blood of Jesus is thicker than the blood of family! When He died on the cross, He took upon His body **all forms** of sickness and disease, including the inherited ones. Therefore, you can exercise authority over the effect or outworking of any hereditary or genetic disorder. As believers in Jesus, we can have peace concerning our health and not fear the diseases of the world.

So if you have received a bad report, don't give up, because it doesn't have to be your final report. Overcome your fears and renew your mind with the truth of what God says regarding your health.

The Past Is Not Your Future!

It is vitally important that you guard what you allow anyone to speak into your life regarding what you are believing for.

> Have nothing to do with godless myths and old wives' tales; rather, train yourself to be godly.
>
> —1 Timothy 4:7

This passage is quite clear in exhorting us not to pay attention to "old wives' tales", myths, folklore or anything contrary to God's Word. There will always be someone willing to share horror stories about their sickness, disease and experiences, or of terrible things that happened to someone they know. You may also have your family sharing their history as well. But know that you don't have to submit to your family's past because the blood of Jesus is thicker than the blood of family!

It is so easy when we hear of someone else's bad experiences to become overwhelmed with fear, imagining that the same things will happen to us. It's important then that you don't allow other peoples' opinions and experiences, or even your own past experiences, to affect the way you view your outcome. Your past, or even their past, is not your future! Instead, meditate on the finished work of the cross so you know what you can experience as a believer in Jesus. Declare what you want to have happen, not what anyone says might happen.

Focus on what God's Word says and listen only to positive testimonies. Your faith will grow through hearing the Word and listening to examples of God's Word in action. In light of this, I suggest that you choose carefully who you share with about the details of what you are believing for. It is hard enough to guard and renew your mind and keep focused on the truth without other people's views and negative remarks working against you. Share only with people who will support and encourage you in your journey. If there isn't anyone, then keep it between yourself and the Lord!

Question 7: *What about my age?*

While we are in this world, God says we are not of this world (2 Corinthians 6:17). We need to remember that Jesus has overcome the world for us. He has deprived it of power to harm us (1 John 5:18, Amp). Regardless of what your situation is, you do not have to be subject to the same concerns as the people of this world. The reality is that age is no barrier when it comes to God's Word and His healing power.

Your Age Is Not An Issue!

If you are faced with a medical prognosis suggesting that your health is greatly reduced due to your age, know that the truth in God's Word is available to **all** who believe in Him. God says that you can be kept fresh and green and still bear fruit into old age.

> The righteous will flourish like a palm tree, they will grow like a cedar of Lebanon; planted in the house of the Lord, they will flourish in the courts of our God. They **will still bear fruit in old age, they will stay fresh and green,** proclaiming, "The Lord is upright; He is my Rock, and there is no wickedness in Him."
>
> —Psalm 92:12–15

If you are concerned about your age affecting your ability to be healthy, then spend time meditating on the truth for a personal revelation, until you see your life through the eyes of what is in the Word and not through your natural eyes and understanding. You must come to a point of agreement with what the Word says and not rely on your natural circumstances. Worrying about your age and your physical condition will keep you focused on the natural realm and the facts, but faith keeps you connected to God's healing power and what you have received through the finished work of the cross.

Absolutely nothing is impossible with God and no Word from God will be without power! God is not a respecter of persons. This means that no matter what your age or your condition, if you believe in Jesus and the truth in His Word, then you already have everything you need in Christ to overcome the natural so you can experience health in your old age!

God does not change. He always remains the same! The only thing that has changed is the times we live in. God does not show favouritism (Romans 2:11), which means that the same breakthrough is available to you today! As we have already seen, if you are in Christ, then healing is already your inheritance. You can exercise authority to walk in that health and be delivered from what is preventing you from walking in perfect health!

Question 8: *What about medical help?*

Let me first state that I have nothing against the medical profession. One of my closest friends, who is on our ministry team in New Life Ministries, is a medical doctor. What I do want to point out though is that medical science can't do everything. I have ministered to many men and women who had been told that there was nothing medical science could do to help them. But while some things are impossible with man, all things are possible with God! Medical science cannot accomplish this, let alone explain it! While they can treat symptoms and sometimes cure sicknesses, they can't form new organs or create living tissue from dead tissue. But God's healing power can!

You may have complications or parts missing in your body and you may be finding it hard to believe God's Word for your healing. If you believe you need medical intervention, it's important that you are aware that while doctors may have the ability to treat your symptoms, they can't do everything. In the gospel of Mark, we see a perfect example of a woman who had spent all she had on doctors and experienced no lasting help.

> And a woman was there who had been subject to bleeding for twelve years. **She had suffered a great deal under the care of many doctors and had spent all she had; yet instead of getting better she grew**

> **worse**. When she heard about Jesus, she came up behind Him in the crowd and touched His cloak, because she thought, "If I just touch His clothes, I will be healed." Immediately her bleeding stopped and she felt in her body that she was freed from her suffering. At once Jesus realised that power had gone out from Him. He turned around in the crowd and asked, "Who touched My clothes?" "You see the people crowding against You," His disciples answered, "and yet You can ask, 'Who touched Me?'" But Jesus kept looking around to see who had done it. Then the woman, knowing what had happened to her, came and fell at His feet and, trembling with fear, told Him the whole truth. He said to her, "**Daughter, your faith has healed you. Go in peace and be freed from your suffering.**"
>
> —Mark 5:25–34

This woman had placed all her hope in the doctors, and in the end they still couldn't help her. She had already spent all that she had and instead of getting better, she grew worse. In the natural, some sicknesses have no cure, so doctors can only treat the symptoms; they often cannot provide lasting help. When it comes to health challenges, some may find themselves losing sight of the power of God and the truth of His Word because of the diagnosis, or the strength of the physical symptoms. It is impossible to focus on what is happening in the natural and focus on the spiritual at the same time. You either look to God and believe His Word or look to your circumstances and believe the diagnosis. There will be times when you will need to continue to walk by what you know to be true according to what God's Word says over what the natural circumstances are. And note that while doctors have your best interest at heart, they don't have all the answers. So if you want real help, just like the woman with the issue of blood, go to Jesus so you can be free from your suffering and be made whole!

> This is what the Lord says: "Cursed is the one who trusts in man, who depends on flesh for his strength and whose heart turns away from the Lord. He will be like a bush in the wastelands; he will not see prosperity when it comes. He will dwell in the parched places of the

> desert, in a salt land where no one lives. **But blessed is the man who trusts in the Lord, whose confidence is in Him.** He will be like a tree planted by the water that sends out its roots by the stream. It does not fear when heat comes; its leaves are always green. It has no worries in a year of drought **and never fails to bear fruit**."
>
> —Jeremiah 17:5–8

Because we have many medical options available to us, it is easy to just go and seek help. However, we need to remember that as believers and followers of Jesus Christ, there is another way. We don't have to run to the doctors, seek treatments or use medications every time we are sick. We can learn to experience healing that we have received from Jesus—the living Word of God.

I made this decision a long time ago. I had enough of always running to the doctors and spending my money on medications. Equally frustrating was the fact that for many of my ailments, there was no known cure or medication available. Having had enough, I began to walk by faith (by what I had received through the finished work of the cross) in different areas of my health. I began with headaches and then worked my way through the various complaints and sicknesses, such as an under-active thyroid, anaemia, bronchitis, viral asthma and allergies. I am now in a place where I do not accept any sickness into my body. At the first sign or symptom, I resist them and the symptoms leave.

You need to be honest with God and with yourself on what you can believe. If you want healing without medical intervention but can't truly believe for that, then you may not be able to walk it out by applying God's Word to your circumstances, and you will only be wasting your time. Go to the Word for a deeper personal revelation on healing. If your decision not to go to the doctor is based on fear of a diagnosis or fear of medical intervention, this may only prolong your situation. Fear is the opposite of faith and you can't walk by faith (by the finished work of the cross) when fearful.

Because modern medicine does not have all the answers, many go down alternative pathways and seek different counsel, such as alternative and holistic medicines and practices in search of an answer. These can often leave an open door for you to become confused and discouraged.

> You are wearied with your many counsels and plans...
>
> —Isaiah 47:13, amp

Suffering with an illness can be a long journey of discouragement, which can often leave you feeling emotionally, and at times also financially, drained. However, whatever report you have received concerning the state of your body, it does not have to be your final report. What has been diagnosed may be factual, but you can't lose if you go to God, because those who look to Him will never be put to shame (Psalm 34:5, Romans 9:33). Be careful, therefore, not to put your trust in a diagnosis, report, scan or test result, because they will keep your focus in the natural realm and can destroy your hope. You need to guard what you allow doctors (or anybody else for that matter) to speak into your life. A diagnosis from a doctor can give a name to what may be affecting your health, but you don't have to submit to that report because it isn't the final authority! Instead, begin to exercise authority over what is preventing you from experiencing and maintaining your healing.

When Shaun was first diagnosed as being sterile, he decided immediately to reject the doctor's prognosis. He wasn't denying the natural facts as they stood because the facts spoke for themselves. But as Shaun sat in that doctor's surgery and was told that medical science could not help him, he knew that he needed to look to God the healer for the solution. And so with his God-given authority, Shaun immediately rejected the condition and the diagnosis of the doctors, and instead chose to trust God. And, praise God, not only was Shaun completely healed, he fathered four children, something medical science said he could never do!

Unfortunately in life, there can be unexpected complications that can arise. For this reason, medical intervention may be required. If this should occur, then remember that God's grace is sufficient for you and you haven't failed if intervention is required. Continue to exercise your authority over the situation and declare that there will be no complications with the procedures and no side effects during the treatment.

While some consider that medical intervention is not God's best, you also need to remember that doctors are there to help God's children, not to harm them. As I have discussed throughout this book, there is a process to learning how to walk by faith and unless we are walking and living by it as a lifestyle, we may not have the confidence to apply it in adverse situations. For this reason, if you know in advance that medical intervention may be required, you can prepare by meditating on the finished work of the cross and on who you are in Christ, and exercise authority over your body and natural circumstances before the doctors proceed with their plans.

Remember always that you have God's Spirit living on the inside of you. Learn how to hear His voice and be led by Him so that He can show you what to do and how to walk in victory.

Question 9: *What do I do when challenged with symptoms of sickness or pain in my body?*

In the world there are many different forms of sickness and disease. But praise God, when you know who you are in Christ, your position in Him and what you have inherited as a believer (all through the finished work of the cross), you will realise that you no longer have to be subject to your body and what state it is in. You can **exercise your authority over any condition** and walk in the healing that Jesus purchased for you.

Remember your authority in Jesus! In the previous chapters, we have seen that we have the same power and authority as Jesus has. We are seated with Christ in heavenly places far above all rule and authority, power and dominion, and every title that can be given, not only in the present age but also in the one to come (Ephesians 1:21; 2:6). So when you face an adverse situation in any area of your life, you can exercise your authority and place the situation under your feet.

A number of years ago, I was diagnosed with an under-active thyroid and was told that I would be on medication for the rest of my life. However, the first report wasn't my last report! I took authority over my body and commanded my thyroid and metabolism to come into line with the truth in God's Word, which said that by Jesus' stripes I was healed. Within a couple of weeks, I experienced complete healing and to this day my thyroid continues to function perfectly.

I have a close friend who was diagnosed with diverticulitis, a condition in the bowel. She would experience severe pain, discomfort and fevers from the recurring infections in her body. She even spent time in hospital on an antibiotic drip after one of the infections. This condition dramatically changed her life and eating habits because she had to eliminate certain foods from her diet. Initially, every time the symptoms began, she would be consumed with fear of what she knew she had to go through. However, she soon learnt how to walk by faith and not by sight, feelings or symptoms in her body. She also learnt to rest in the finished work of the cross, knowing that Jesus had already paid the price for her healing of this condition. Every time the symptoms began, she would exercise authority over her body by resisting the pain, infection and fear. She would also declare what Jesus had done by confessing that by His stripes she was healed! While initially she had to exercise her authority daily over the condition, she soon began to renew her mind and see the condition in another light. Not long after this, a colonoscopy revealed that there was absolutely nothing wrong with her bowel! She was healed! And to this day she is able to eat normally and enjoy her healing!

What are you facing in your body right now? Don't put up with it any longer; simply take authority over it! Command your body to get into perfect working order and to function the way God designed it to.

Regardless of your condition, you have authority over your own body. Don't allow it to be the other way around! If you exercise authority and command any form of sickness to be removed, then it must be removed. If you tell it to die at the root, then it will die at the root. If you resist it, then it must flee! Even cancer must flee when you resist it!

The majority of the people I minister to are in a desperate situation. They have usually tried every avenue and like the account of the woman with the issue of blood in the Gospels, instead of getting better, they have grown worse. But through the truth of God's Word, they discover that they don't have to live under or with their diagnosis, because they can exercise their authority over any condition in their bodies and experience healing. Consequently, there have been many amazing testimonies all around the world from those who have received breakthroughs.

When you begin to exercise authority over your body (or your situation), start with what you can believe right now. While absolutely nothing is impossible, sometimes there are mindsets in place that highly regard the size or type of the condition. We live in a world that almost glorifies illness, so sometimes your mind will consider your condition according to what the natural circumstances are, or on the strength of what your diagnosis is. You may also feel that you have to accept certain conditions due to your past, your genetic makeup or your age. Remember that Jesus has already paid the price for the healing of ALL forms of sickness and disease! Why then should we allow our bodies to function with an imbalance? Why put up with anything less than perfect order in our bodies? Continue to meditate on this truth until you see your condition through the eyes of the finished work of the cross, and the natural facts lose their power. In order to begin to learn how to exercise your authority and experience healing, I suggest you focus on walking by faith in healing by beginning with areas that may require healing. Start somewhere and continue to walk by faith, not by sight or appearance, and exercise your authority until your breakthrough is realised.

Question 10: *Why do I need to speak to my body and take authority over it?*

I sometimes get asked, "How often should I speak to my body?" I do not believe that there is a right or wrong way when it comes to how many times you should speak to your body. As I have noted previously, my intention is never to present a formula for you to follow to attain your desired result, because it is not about works or doing something to earn your breakthrough. From both personal experience and from observation, following "steps" without revelation is not only powerless but also leads to frustration. As we have already discovered, you have already received the victory you need upon your salvation. Healing is already your provision. So you don't exercise authority over your body to get God to do what Jesus has already done! Instead, you are exercising your God-given authority over your natural circumstances to put a stop to them outworking in your life, and to enable you to walk in the healing that already belongs to you.

When I first received the revelation of the power and authority I had in Jesus, I would exercise authority over any symptom of sickness every time I had a concern about it or felt a symptom. I found that this kept me focused on the truth in God's Word and not on what the natural circumstances were doing. Initially, this was a continual process until my mind was renewed and I saw the condition through the eyes of God's Word and not through my natural understanding. I was determined not to let go of what I believed to be the truth. While initially it took time before I saw change in the natural symptoms (even when I applied this to a sore throat or a common cold), I now see more immediate results.

It can take time to renew our mind and truly believe what Jesus has already done. And it also takes time to learn not to walk by what the natural symptoms or circumstances are doing. It is so easy to give in, but when you continue to walk by faith and exercise authority over the natural situation, then changes do begin to take place. Therefore, I want to encourage you not to become disheartened if you don't see instant results. If after a while however, there are no signs of improvement, then I suggest you seek God and go back to His Word for a fresh revelation. Also, one question I would ask: **Do you expect your body to respond when you command it to change**? If you simply speak over your body and hope for the best, then you will only be deceiving yourself. You need to know and believe in your heart that you have the same power and authority as Jesus. Say, "NO! Body, you are to bow down to the name and authority of Jesus," and then tell it what to do. I would suggest that you keep focused and continue until you do see change.

Question 11: *Isn't making confessions "works" and legalistic?*

When you become a Christian, you don't have to remind yourself to say the right thing and speak about Jesus do you? No! When your heart has been changed, you automatically speak it out. The Bible says that out of the abundance of the heart the mouth speaks (Luke 6:45, NKJV). Whatever is coming out of your mouth is usually what is in your heart. Faith is not just mere confession, but a knowing in your spirit (it is believing in Jesus). When you know something, you can't help but speak it out! Your conversation simply lines up with what you believe. For this reason, if you get into fear about your confession or about saying the wrong thing, then it can easily become legalistic.

Confession (which means "to agree with" or "say the same thing as") is not about how many times you pray or speak the Word. Repetition and the number of prayers do not bring the Word to pass. Jesus has already paid the price for the healing of all sicknesses in your body. You can't earn or work for it because it is a free gift. We simply need to walk in our inheritance by applying this truth to our daily lives. Remember that God released His power by what He said. His Words framed and fashioned what He desired and the natural realm submitted and responded to His power. We need to remember that the power of God's kingdom is dwelling on the inside of us through the Holy Spirit. We also have God's will, plan and purpose already established in His Word through the work Jesus did on the cross.

If we want to see this truth become a reality in our lives, then we need to know, believe and act on the truth by opening our mouths and exercising God's power and authority over the natural hindrances and circumstances that are preventing God's plan from being fulfilled in our lives. This is not trying to get God to do something for us, but laying hold of what He has already done!

Take God's Medicine

TWELVE

If you are challenged with any form of sickness or disease, remind yourself of the finished work of the cross. Jesus became a curse for you. He took your place and every curse was laid upon Him, and you are now free. Therefore, it's important to put more faith in what God says than in what your symptoms, diagnosis or the doctors say.

If your doctor gives you a medical diagnosis or prognosis and you believe it, then you will begin to plan your life based on the doctor's report. But what does God say? The Bible says that the Word of God is *the* truth and when you know that truth, it will set you free. Believe God's truth in spite of the doctor's report and act accordingly. Begin to meditate on and take God's Word as medicine into your heart so that you can see the outworking of what Jesus has purchased for you become reality in your life!

> My son, **attend to my words**; consent and submit to my sayings [The KJV says...incline thine ear unto my sayings]. Let them not depart from your sight; **keep them** in the centre of your heart. For they are life to those who find them, healing and **health** to all their flesh. **Keep and guard your heart with all vigilance** and above all that you guard, for out of it flow the springs of life. [The NIV says...guard your heart, for it is the wellspring of life].
>
> —Proverbs 4:20–23, AMP

If we want to have the "springs of life" flowing out of our hearts, affecting our bodies, minds and outward circumstances, then we need to keep God's Word before our eyes and ears by reading it, meditating upon it, hearing it preached and hearing our own voices speaking it. God's Word is alive and full of power (Hebrews 4:12). Think about it: When you keep meditating on something that's alive and full of power, it has to bring **healing and health** to your flesh!

The word "health" in Proverbs 4:22 means "cure" or "remedy". God's Word is the cure, remedy or the **medicine** that we take to receive healing in our physical bodies and bring life to our outward circumstances! If you went to a doctor and he prescribed medication for you to take three times a day, would you take it? Of course you would. You would take it in faith expecting it to cure you. Since God's power is greater than any worldly medicine, it will not only cure the symptoms, but it can also bring healing to what was causing the condition in the first place. **Now that is good news!**

Meditate on the following truths in God's Word, allowing time for them to penetrate into your heart so that they will bring life to your outward circumstances and healing and health to your flesh. Continue to renew your mind with them and make them personal to you by speaking them out as a confession over your life.

What God Says...

...For I am the Lord, who heals you.

—Exodus 15:26

Worship the Lord your God, and His blessing will be on your food and water. **I will take away sickness from among you**, and none will miscarry or be barren in your land. I will give you a full life span.

—Exodus 23:25–26

Then your light will break forth like the dawn, and your healing will quickly appear; then your righteousness will go before you, and the glory of the Lord will be your rear guard.

—Isaiah 58:8

But for you who revere My name, the sun of righteousness will rise with healing in its wings. And you will go out and leap like calves released from the stall.

—Malachi 4:2

"Nevertheless, I will bring health and healing to it; I will heal My people and will let them enjoy abundant peace and security."

—Jeremiah 33:6

"But I will restore you to health and heal your wounds," declares the Lord...

—Jeremiah 30:17

But those who suffer He delivers in their suffering; He speaks to them in their affliction.

—Job 36:15

And the prayer offered in faith will make the sick person well; the Lord will raise him up. If he has sinned, he will be forgiven.

—James 5:15

What You Can Say...

Let the redeemed of the Lord say so! Begin to make the following scriptural confessions over your life!

I am blessed. (Deuteronomy 2:7, Matthew 5:3–10; 13:16)

I am fearfully and wonderfully made. (Psalm 139:14)

He sent forth His Word and healed me. (Psalm 107:20)

Christ has redeemed me from the curse of the law by becoming a curse for me, for it is written: "Cursed is everyone who is hung on a tree." Therefore, I AM redeemed from every form of sickness and disease! (Galatians 3:13)

Jesus ***has borne*** *my griefs* ***(sicknesses, weaknesses and distresses) and carried*** *my* ***sorrows*** *and pains (of punishment). He was wounded for my transgressions, He was bruised for my guilt and iniquities. The chastisement (needful to obtain) peace and well-being for me was upon Him, and with the stripes that wounded* ***Him I am healed and made whole.*** (Isaiah 53:4–5, AMP)

Jesus bore my sins in His body on the tree. I am now dead to sin, and I live unto righteousness: by His ***stripes*** *I was* ***healed.*** (1 Peter 2:24, NKJV)

Because of Jesus I am restored to health and healed from all my wounds. (Jeremiah 30:17)

The joy of the Lord is my strength. (Psalm 28:7, Nehemiah 8:10)

I praise the Lord with all my soul and I forget not all His benefits: HE HAS ***forgiven all*** *my sins and* ***healed ALL my diseases.*** *He has redeemed my life from the pit and crowned me with love and compassion.* (Psalm 103:2–4)

Jesus has taken sickness from me. Therefore, I will not be barren or miscarry. I will also have a full life span. (Exodus 23:25–26)

I HAVE BEEN DELIVERED, HEALED, SET FREE AND MADE WHOLE. (Isaiah 53:5, Matthew 8:16–17)

Healing Prayer And Declaration

I bind Satan's power over my body and I resist ALL forms of sickness, disease, pain and complications and I command you to leave!

Jesus bore my sickness, disease and pain in my place so I can be set free.

I am redeemed from the curse of the law.

Therefore, I command my body in Jesus' name to come in line with the Word of God and to behave healed. Body, you are to function the way God created you to—perfectly and efficiently because you are fearfully and wonderfully made. You are to function in perfect working order.

I walk in victory over sickness and disease and I declare in Jesus' name that I AM healed and made whole.

Amen!

No More Pain!

THIRTEEN

We have already discovered that when God created Adam and Eve in the Garden of Eden, they were perfect—fearfully and wonderfully made. We have also seen that when God looked over all His creation, He saw that it was very good (Genesis 1:31). Sickness, disease, pain and complications did not exist. They were introduced into this world after the fall of Adam and Eve. Adam and Eve were now living in a fallen world where sin had been conceived and had given birth to death. Pain, along with sickness, disease and other complications had also entered and the consequence was that they were now open to experience any part of these manifestations.

Redeemed From Pain

As we saw in the previous chapter, Deuteronomy 28:16–68 details all of the curses under the law of sin and death. This extensive list of sicknesses, diseases and complications were what came into this world through sin and they still exist today. But God sent Jesus to reverse the curse and to set us free from all the effects of sin.

> Christ has redeemed us from the curse of the law by becoming a curse for us, for it is written: "Cursed is everyone who is hung on a tree."
>
> —Galatians 3:13

This means that we have been redeemed from **every** part of the curse of the law, and this includes all forms of sickness, disease, pain and complications mentioned within it. It doesn't matter what form the pain comes in. Whether it's the pain of childbirth, a toothache, headache, backache, physical injury, or even emotional and mental pain, we have been redeemed from them all.

For the most part, pain is the body's response to an underlying cause. But this doesn't mean that we accept it as "par for the course". No matter what the cause, pain is under the curse of the law, and because we are redeemed from the curse, it no longer has any legal right to afflict us!

We have been legally set free from all of these consequences of sin. Jesus took the full force of sin, and as a result took the fruit of sin such as sickness, disease and pain of every kind. The price for our redemption from all of this was paid for in full. Thank God for the finished work of the cross!

Jesus Carried Our Pains Away!

> Surely He **took up** our **infirmities** and **carried** our **sorrows**, yet we considered Him stricken by God, smitten by Him, and afflicted. But He was pierced for our transgressions, He was crushed for our iniquities; the punishment that brought us peace was upon Him, and by His wounds we **are** healed.
>
> —Isaiah 53:4–5

We read in the previous chapter that the word "infirmities" in the scripture above is the Hebrew word *choli,* which means, sickness, disease, grief, sick. The word "sorrows" is the Hebrew word *makob*, which means, **pain**, grief, and that word "pain" is further described as, sorrow (emotional), pain (physical), pain (mental).

Therefore, Isaiah 53:4–5 should correctly read, "Jesus took up all our **sicknesses, diseases and griefs**, and carried our sorrows **and physical, emotional and mental pains** away!" Remember, Jesus took all forms of sickness, disease, grief, sorrow, distress and pain upon His body on the cross in our place!

The Amplified Bible of Isaiah 53:3–5 says it this way:

> He was despised and rejected and forsaken by men, a Man of sorrows and pains, and acquainted with grief and sickness; and like one from whom men hide their faces He was despised, and we did not appreciate His worth or have any esteem for Him. Surely **He has borne our griefs (sicknesses, weaknesses, and distresses) and carried our sorrows and pains** [of punishment], yet we [ignorantly] considered Him stricken, smitten, and afflicted by God [as if with leprosy]. But He was wounded for our transgressions, He was bruised for our guilt and iniquities; the chastisement [needful to obtain] peace and well-being for us was upon Him, and with the stripes [that wounded] Him **we are healed and made whole**.

When I discovered the truth that Jesus took sickness, pain and sorrow in my place, I began to apply it to every area of my life. It didn't matter what form the sickness or pain came in, whether it was chronic pain, headaches, toothaches, sporting injuries or even childbirth pains! Once I discovered what Jesus had done, I then needed to apply that truth, because it sure wasn't manifesting on knowledge alone!

I received a deeper revelation of the fullness of what Jesus had done on the cross when I once experienced a bad case of stomach cramps. The pain from the cramps was unbearable. I remember being in so much pain that I cried out, "Jesus, help me." What happened next was amazing! I had a vision of Jesus' hand coming down and resting on my abdomen. As this happened, the awareness of the pain I was experiencing left my body. I could tell that my body was still cramping, but my stomach had gone numb. There was no pain! I rebuked the sickness that was causing the condition and the cramps completely stopped. I walked away instantly healed. Jesus had carried all the pain from my body. He took the full force of it away! This is what Jesus had done on the cross and this vision helped me to see that truth become a reality in my life.

Now, whenever I experience any form of pain, I focus on what Jesus has done and take authority over the pain, and each time the pain wanes and disappears.

I caution you to not fall into presumption. You will need to spend the time renewing your mind with the truth and seeking God for a personal revelation of the fact that you don't have to suffer with any pain. Remember, it will not manifest on knowledge alone. Information needs to become revelation for you to experience healing by acting on what you believe and by taking authority over the natural symptoms.

When you understand this truth, you will realise that you don't have to suffer or be traumatised with any form of pain because Jesus paid the price for this too. So you can now apply this truth to expect a completely different outcome! If you find that when you experience pain that it becomes too strong or unbearable and you need to take medication to ease the pain, then do so, but don't give up! Continue to focus on Jesus and the finished work of the cross. This will enable you to receive fresh revelation and stay in the place of rest. Then, when the medication kicks in you will be in a better position to exercise authority over the physical symptoms and resist the pain. Remember always that you haven't failed if you need help along the way. Start where you are at now and let the Holy Spirit guide and lead you into the breakthrough you need every step of the way! That way, you will find yourself growing from faith to faith, from strength to strength, and from glory to glory!

Beat The Blues!

FOURTEEN

Feeling sad is a perfectly normal human emotion that we will all experience from time to time. Depression, however, is very different from the emotion of sadness. Depression is when the sufferer experiences persistent feelings of gloom or sadness that persist for weeks or even months.

There are different types of depression and it will be unique to every sufferer. It can be mild and short-lived, but for others, depression can descend like a black cloud and remain for a long period of time.

My Story

After I gave birth to my first child, my whole body, including my hormones and emotions, were out of balance. My thyroid gland was under-active and I gained 15kg within three months. My baby was also unsettled. I was struggling with insomnia and I was an emotional mess. I would go from happy to sad to angry within minutes, and was irrational over insignificant events. There was a time where I actually cried over spilt milk! I was also experiencing the same symptoms as an older friend who was menopausal. I would become dizzy and lose balance. I had hair growth under my chin and I experienced hot and cold flushes and skin crawls, to name just a few symptoms.

Spiritually, I felt like I was in a dark pit. I had no energy and if I tried to pray, all I could put together was, "Jesus, help me." It would then feel like a lid would come down and stop my prayer. I couldn't concentrate on anything. Even when I tried to read my Bible, I would read the same line over and over again. I was oppressed and depressed. I tried to cope on my own for eight weeks before seeking help. I was referred to a doctor and was diagnosed with postnatal depression. Medically, there was no solution given to me apart from anti-depressants. While I was initially diagnosed with postnatal depression, after I received healing and recognized the symptoms, I realised that I had suffered with depression on and off for most of my life.

I praise God for what His Son, Jesus Christ, did on the cross for me! I received my breakthrough at a women's group meeting soon after. For several weeks, they had prayed for inner strength for me but the week they took authority over the depression was when the victory came! I felt the oppression and depression break and lift off while I was being prayed for. Finally, the darkness was gone. Everything had been dull and dreary but was now bursting with colour again. However, I had to continue to walk by faith and exercise my authority to maintain my healing. At first, it felt like I was in an intense spiritual battle. I had to renew my mind by gaining some order and discipline in my thought life. I researched scriptures on the renewal of my mind and on my position in Christ. I meditated on them and applied them by declaring what they said aloud whenever I felt challenged. I also commanded the depression to go away. I continued to do this every time the familiar thoughts or feelings of depression started to creep in, and they would flee!

This battle was constant at first but I soon grew stronger as my mind was being renewed in the truth of God's Word. I found that I was able to walk by what God said about me in His Word and not by how I was feeling at the time. I discovered that even though my feelings, emotions and thoughts were real, I didn't have to submit to and live under them. Instead, I began to exercise my authority over them and place my feelings, emotions and thoughts into submission to God's Word. As the truth in the Word became established in my heart, the strength of the depression abated and in only a short period of time, I was able to walk in complete victory. My life had turned around. Instead of being a victim enslaved by my feelings, emotions and thought-life, I became the victor!

I continued to walk by what God's Word said and exercised authority over my emotions, hormones, feelings and moods. And since then at no point has depression ever had a hold on me. I was able to recognise the symptoms and that enabled me to oppose them at the onset so I was able to maintain the victory, peace and the joy of the Lord. When I was set free, I was free indeed.

There Is Light At The End Of The Tunnel!

One thing I noticed while I was suffering from depression was that no one talked about it. I kept thinking that there was something wrong with me because it seemed like I was the only one with a problem. Someone who is struggling with depression may feel condemned and unable to ask for help if they perceive that everyone else is coping with life and they're not. They may also feel alienated and a failure. Because of this, many suffer alone needlessly. I experienced this, but I later found that many others had felt the same way, but were either too embarrassed or too proud to talk about it. You don't have to "tell all" to everyone who asks, but if you're feeling overwhelmed, it will be comforting to know that you are not alone. I have come to realise, especially among Christians, that there is an expectation that everyone should be coping and to appear otherwise is judged as a sign of weakness and spiritual immaturity. However, this could not be further from the truth. Remember, there is no condemnation in Christ Jesus! The Bible tells us to love, support and encourage one another with prayer. Depression sufferers especially need this type of support and encouragement.

Depression should never be kept to yourself because to suppress or ignore it will only make matters worse. It can be a very serious condition if left unattended. To admit you have a problem is not a sign of weakness or failure, but of strength and courage. It is also the first step to recovery. It's important that you understand that there is absolutely nothing to be ashamed of. There is light at the end of the tunnel and there is nothing wrong if you need help to get there.

It's also important to know that you haven't failed if you need to seek medical advice or take medication such as anti-depressants. For some sufferers, the medication helps them to cope with life again. This in turn might provide them with the strength to focus and begin to walk by faith in the Word (through the finished work of the cross) to overcome their depression. It's important to note, however, that when doctors treat depression sufferers with medication such as anti-depressants or tranquilisers, they are only numbing their emotions. They cannot heal them, so the thoughts, feelings and the root of the depression will still be there. Medication can only ever reach the physical, not the spiritual realm. And while psychologists, psychiatrists or counsellors work with the mind and help with past issues, only Jesus can heal the soul, and help you to **overcome** depression, unbalanced emotions or other torments of the mind.

Remember that when you received your salvation, you received everything you need to walk in victory in every area of life. So if you are experiencing any form of depression or imbalance in your body, know that healing is already available! The inheritance you received for forgiveness of sins and healing in your physical body is the same inheritance that provides healing power that can heal and transform your thought life and emotions so that you can be whole—spirit, soul and body!

Hormones, Feelings And Emotions

Well-balanced hormones in our body and chemicals in our brains play a significant role in our health. Hormones are chemical messengers that dictate how our body behaves. They can also control the way we feel emotionally.

I had blood tests that showed that my hormone levels were out of balance. I experienced mood swings and I was over-sensitive. All the "mole hills" seemed like huge mountains in my life. I took everything to heart and was easily offended. Even though some of my concerns were valid, my irrational behaviour was out of balance. In addition, I would constantly worry about different things that were said to me and I would dwell on what I imagined could happen in the future. My thought life was out of control! I believe all of these things played a major role in my progressive spiral into suffering with depression.

However, I soon learnt that I didn't have to be subject to my hormones or emotions, because I had authority over my own thought life, feelings, emotions and body. I needed to turn things around because my body, including my thoughts and emotions, had been controlling me! I had to learn to walk by the Word and live by the Spirit—not by my flesh or feelings. I reminded myself that I was a temple of the Holy Spirit and I needed to be a wise steward of the body and thought-life that God had given me. I meditated on scriptures to renew my mind on who I was in Christ. I then walked that out by taking authority over my hormones, emotions and feelings, and declared the truth in God's Word instead. Praise God, I soon experienced freedom over worry, mood swings, emotional outbursts and depression!

I used to always say, "I can't help how I feel," but in reality, the opposite is true! While we may feel a certain way, **we can choose** not to let our feelings and emotions dictate how we are going to behave! Our feelings and emotions are not bad in themselves. It is how we respond to them that matters. Remember, the truth is that your feelings are always subject to change—**you are not subject to your feelings**! When I discovered this truth, I began to live daily in the peace of God, free from emotional stress and worry, experiencing the joy of the Lord as my strength!

The Complete Work Of The Cross

At the end of the day, depression is just another form of sickness. Depression has no legal right to stay or have the victory over you any longer. Jesus took ALL forms of sickness and disease to the cross and by His stripes you were healed!

> Surely He took up our **infirmities** and carried our **sorrows**, yet we considered Him stricken by God, smitten by Him, and afflicted.
> But He was pierced for our transgressions, He was crushed for our iniquities; the punishment that brought us peace was upon Him, and by His wounds we **are** healed.
>
> —Isaiah 53:4–5

Earlier, I covered the meaning of the word "**sorrows**" (*makob*), which in this scripture is defined as, sorrow, pain and grief. Pain in this context means pain in the form of sorrow, physical pain as well as mental or emotional pain.

The dictionary definitions of these words are best described as follows and show the fullness of what Jesus purchased for us:

Pain: bodily or mental suffering, distress, trouble, exertion.

Sorrow: pain of mind, grief, sadness, distress, cause of grief, to feel pain of mind, to grieve, sad, unhappy.

Grief: deep sorrow, pain, the cause of sorrow or distress.

This means that along with our sins, sicknesses and diseases, Jesus carried the full force of our griefs, sorrows, physical, mental and emotional pains and sufferings on the cross—in our place! He provided healing of the whole person—spirit, soul and body. By Jesus' stripes you have been healed and made whole!

Satan has no legal right to torment you mentally (unless you allow it). You have been redeemed from fear, anxiety and depression and from anything else that steals your peace of mind. We **have been given** a spirit of power, love and a sound mind (1 Timothy 4:7). We don't have to rely on anti-depressants, medications or any tranquillisers to help us cope with life or to receive peace of mind. By applying the finished work of the cross to this area of your life, you can overcome depression and walk in lasting victory.

Cast Your Cares!

> Casting the whole of your care [all your anxieties, all your worries, all your concerns, once and for all] on Him, for He cares for you affectionately and cares about you watchfully.
>
> —1 Peter 5:7, amp

The word "casting" means, to fling, throw, shed, or hurl, to not hold onto. Jesus cast out demons, men cast nets and we need to cast our cares to the Lord. God didn't create us to be burdened with life's issues or with the cares of the world. Whatever you focus on (pay attention to by worrying, analysing or thinking upon), you give it power and a hold on your life. So make the decision to let them go and focus instead on who God is and His love for you.

Maintaining Your Healing

> It is for freedom that Christ has set us free. Stand firm, then, and do

> not let yourselves be burdened again by a yoke of slavery.
>
> —Galatians 5:1

If you begin to experience familiar feelings, thoughts or symptoms of depression, this doesn't mean that you haven't been healed. You simply need to exercise authority and resist the symptoms to continue to experience lasting victory. When Jesus set you free, you were free indeed! Therefore, don't give the enemy or your natural feelings and thought-life the opportunity to deceive you into submitting to the old state of mind.

You Have ALREADY Been Delivered!

> [The Father] **has delivered** and drawn us to Himself **out of the control and the dominion of darkness** and has transferred us into the kingdom of the Son of His love, in whom we have our redemption through His blood, [which means] the forgiveness of our sins.
>
> —Colossians 1:13–14, amp

There's no need for an extensive deliverance ministry when it comes to depression. The truth is that you have already been delivered from the control and dominion of the enemy! You can walk in and maintain your freedom every day because Jesus has already obtained the victory over depression and spiritual oppression! Many who suffer depression have an unrenewed mind and struggle with fear, worry, anxiety or from events of the past. They are easy targets for Satan's torment. Always remember the truth of who you are in Christ so that you can overcome your fears and the lies of the enemy.

Therefore, continue to walk by the finished work of the cross and the fullness of what Jesus has done for you by applying this truth to every area of your life. If you begin to experience symptoms of any kind (physical, emotional or mental), resist them at the onset! Declare the truth of what God's Word says about you and your situation, and continue to guard your mind and what you allow yourself to think and focus upon. While the battle may seem constant at first, soon you will be strong enough to walk in complete victory!

God's Medicine For Depression

> He heals the brokenhearted and binds up their wounds. He determines the number of the stars and calls them each by name. Great is our Lord and mighty in power; His understanding has no limit.
>
> —Psalm 147:3–5

By Jesus' stripes **you have been** healed. Therefore, if you begin to experience any symptoms of any kind (physical, emotional or mental) you can resist them at the onset! Continue to declare the truth of what God's Word says about you and continue to guard your mind and what you allow yourself to think and focus upon.

> The Lord gives strength to His people; the Lord blesses His people with peace.
>
> —Psalm 29:11

> He gives strength to the weary and increases the power of the weak... but those who hope in the Lord will renew their strength. They will soar on wings like eagles; they will run and not grow weary, they will walk and not be faint.
>
> —Isaiah 40:29, 31

> So do not fear, for I am with you; do not be dismayed, for I am your God. I will strengthen you and help you; I will uphold you with My righteous right hand...For I am the Lord, your God, who takes hold of your right hand and says to you, "Do not fear; I will help you."
>
> —Isaiah 41:10, 13

> ...be satisfied with your present [circumstances and with what you have]; for He [God] Himself has said, "I will not in any way fail you nor give you up nor leave you without support. [I will] not, [I will] not, [I will] not in any degree leave you helpless nor forsake nor let [you] down (relax My hold on you)! [Assuredly not!]"
>
> —Hebrews 13:5, amp

What You Can Say...

Let the redeemed of the Lord say so! Begin to make the following scriptural confessions over your life!

> *God is my refuge and strength, an ever-present help in trouble.* (Psalm 46:1)
>
> *I pray that out of His glorious riches, I will be strengthened with power through His Spirit in my inner being, because Christ dwells in my heart through faith. And I pray that I will be rooted and established in His love and have power, to grasp how wide and long and high and deep is the love of Christ, and to know this love that surpasses knowledge, that I may be filled to the measure of all the fullness of God.* (Ephesians 3:16–19)
>
> *The Father* ***has delivered*** *and drawn me to Himself out of the control and the dominion of darkness and* ***has transferred*** *me into the kingdom of the Son of His love, in whom I have redemption through His blood, which means the forgiveness of my sins.* (Colossians 1:13–14, AMP)
>
> *The Spirit of the Sovereign Lord is on me, because the Lord has anointed me to preach good news to the poor. He has sent me to bind up the broken-hearted, to proclaim freedom for the captives and release from darkness for the prisoners, to proclaim the year of the Lord's favour and the day of vengeance of our God, to comfort all who mourn, and provide for those who grieve in Zion—to bestow on them a crown of beauty instead of ashes, the oil of gladness instead of mourning, and a* ***garment of praise instead of a spirit of despair.*** (Isaiah 61:1–3)
>
> *I am restored to health and healed from all my wounds.* (Jeremiah 30:17)
>
> *I will be anxious for nothing, but in everything I'll let my requests be made known to God. And the peace of God, which surpasses all understanding, shall guard my heart and mind through Christ Jesus.*

I will only think on things that are true, honest, just, pure, lovely, and are of a good report. (Philippians 4:6–8)

I am strong in the Lord. I am empowered through my union with Him. I draw my strength from Him, that strength which His boundless might provides. (Ephesians 6:10, AMP)

I have strength for all things in Christ who empowers me. I am ready for anything and equal to anything through Him who infuses inner strength into me. I am self-sufficient in Christ's sufficiency. (Philippians 4:13, AMP)

It is God who arms me with strength and makes my way perfect. (2 Samuel 22:33)

Leaving The Past In The Past!

FIFTEEN

I have found that besides physical healing, many also seek healing for emotional issues that have arisen from the effects of what they have experienced in their past. This is an area where many remain captive and struggle to break free. But there is good news for anyone wanting freedom from their past. The work that Jesus did on the cross was complete, and the price He paid is enough for you to walk in victory in every area of your life!

The Real Battle

The Bible tells us that we are not to be ignorant of the devil's schemes. So when it comes to overcoming our past, it is important to understand where the real battle lies so that the weapons of our adversary will not overwhelm or deceive us. I believe that guilt, shame and condemnation are weapons used to tie us to the past in an attempt to ruin our future. They limit how we relate to God, causing us to feel unworthy to come before Him with a clean conscience.

However, it is important to note that while we have an adversary, he is not always behind what we feel or experience. If we continue to live out of our natural feelings, emotions, senses and understanding, then we can remain bound in our own thinking. Additionally, if we don't walk by the truth of who we are in Christ, then our natural man will continue to govern how we think, feel, react and behave.

When we understand what God has done through the finished work of the cross, we can break free from the chains that are holding us back so that we can experience lasting wholeness and freedom over the past. Therefore, we need to learn how to walk by the truth of who we are in Christ so that His life and power can heal and transform how we feel and how we see and express ourselves.

For many years, the guilt, shame and condemnation of some things I had done in my past prevented me from experiencing God's unconditional love, approval and acceptance. But when I began to discover the truth of who I was in Christ, I found that these feelings were all lies and deceptions! I also learnt that while I was unable to change the past, I could change what happens today and put a stop to the effects or outworking of what happened in the days gone by. So I began to renew my mind and walk by the truth of what God's Word said and soon the pain, shame and guilt lost their power. Praise God, my past is now a distant memory.

Regardless of what we go through, we need to always remember the truth about Satan—the battle has already been won and he has already been defeated. Through the work that Jesus did on the cross, He disarmed and deprived the devil of the power to harm us. So when you know who you are in Christ, you will realise that you no longer need to struggle with anything from your past because Satan's power and hold over you **has**

already been broken (Colossians 1:13–14). Did you know that because Satan is a defeated foe, the only power he has in your life is what you allow him to have? If he can deceive you into believing his lies, then that is how he gains power and control in your life. So get to know the truth about guilt, shame, condemnation and how God sees your past so that you can walk in victory and experience the fullness of what God has provided for you today.

Unworthiness Is A Big Fat Lie!

The dictionary definition of "unworthy" is, not deserving a particular benefit, privilege, or compliment, and lacking value or merit. If we don't believe that we are worthy to come before God, we will be deceived into feeling shameful, not good enough or undeserving to receive from God. Satan wants us to continue to feel unworthy because he knows that it will prevent us from having bold faith and confidence in God and His Word.

We need to know the truth and realise that **unworthiness is a big fat lie!** Through the complete and finished work of the cross, God has already made us worthy—righteous, blameless, loved, accepted and approved!

> Praise be to the God and Father of our Lord Jesus Christ, **who has blessed** us in the heavenly realms with every spiritual blessing in Christ. For He chose us in Him before the creation of the world **to be holy and blameless in His sight**. In love He predestined us to be **adopted as His sons** through Jesus Christ, in accordance with His pleasure and will—to the praise of His glorious grace, which He has freely given us in the One He loves. In Him **we have redemption through His blood, the forgiveness of sins**, in accordance with the **riches of God's grace that He lavished on us** with all wisdom and understanding.
>
> —Ephesians 1:3–8

If you are in Christ then there is nothing that you can do that will make you more or less righteous, loved, approved or accepted in God's eyes, because we cannot earn favour from God. God's grace is not dependent on us and on our performance—on what we can do. The promises of God are a **free gift** and have already been given to those who by faith have a relationship with Jesus! This means that if you are in Christ, then what Jesus purchased for you on the cross is already your inheritance! You received it all upon your salvation!

> For it is by **free grace** (God's unmerited favour) that you are saved (delivered from judgment and made partakers of Christ's salvation) through [your] faith. And this [salvation] is not of yourselves [of your own doing, it came not through your own striving], but it is **the gift of God**; not because of works [not the fulfilment of the law's demands], lest any man should boast. [It is not the result of what anyone can possibly do, so no one can pride himself in it or take glory to himself.]
>
> —Ephesians 2:8–9, amp

By grace you have been saved (forgiven, healed, delivered, set free and made whole), through faith. It is not by your own faith you receive, BUT **because you have faith in Jesus** you have already received! **This is what grace is about**! We cannot do one thing to earn God's favour; it is a free gift lavished on us because of God's great love for us.

Jesus has paid the price and penalty for all our sins. So through Jesus we have been set free from sin and all its punishment! This includes unworthiness and all the guilt, shame and condemnation that cause this. This means that our right standing with God and freedom from our past are not dependant on what we can do to make things right, but are all dependent on Jesus and what **He has already purchased** for us!

Guilt And Shame

> "Do not be afraid; you will not suffer shame. Do not fear disgrace; you will not be humiliated. You will forget the shame of your youth..."
>
> —Isaiah 54:4

I have ministered to many believers who struggle with guilt or shame. Some believe that God is the one who is constantly highlighting and exposing the sins of their past. But nothing could be further from the truth! Do you think that a loving Father that has already forgiven and cleansed us would then make us feel dirty or worthless? Of course not! The truth is that Satan, **not God**, is the accuser of the brethren and is behind all the guilt, shame and condemnation. He is the one who comes to torment you with guilt to make you feel guilty and ashamed of your past (Revelation 12:10).

In order to walk in freedom over guilt and shame, we need to know the truth of what they are and why they continue to torment us. Guilt arises as a result of committing an offense or having done something wrong because of sin. It produces inward feelings of regret, remorse, shame and feelings of failure, leaving us with a guilty conscience and condemnation, which is "the need to punish" ourselves. This can also drive us into "works" or self-effort where we try to earn favour with God through our performance. However, the good news is that Jesus paid the price and penalty for **all our sins** through His finished work at the cross. Jesus came and offered Himself as the atoning sacrifice for sin and in doing so He satisfied the wrath of God (the punishment of sin) for all mankind. So for those who belong to Jesus, the truth is that there is no longer any punishment for sin!

> ...He was wounded **for our transgressions**, He was bruised **for our iniquities**; the chastisement **for our peace** was **upon Him**, and by His stripes we are healed.
>
> —ISAIAH 53:5, NKJV

God does not punish us, so we need to stop punishing ourselves! God **has forgiven** and cleansed us from sin, so we need to forgive ourselves too! But as long as we keep meditating on and reminding ourselves of what happened in the past, we will continue to give power to the devil in that area. While we cannot change what happened in the past we can change what happens today! Therefore, we need to renew our minds and apply this truth until the guilt and pain of the memory caused by our sin (or from the sin of others against us) lose their power and hold over our lives. We have been given a free will with the power to choose! So make the decision to choose to forgive yourself for what you did or said (or even what happened to you) thereby robbing Satan of his power over your life through shame and guilt.

> But if we [really] are living and walking in the Light, as He [Himself] is in the Light, we have [true, unbroken] fellowship with one another, and the blood of Jesus Christ His Son cleanses (removes) us from **all sin and guilt** [keeps us cleansed from sin **in all its forms and manifestations**].
>
> —1 John 1:7, AMP

Did you know that in the new covenant the word "guilt" is not mentioned in regards to sin and the believer? This is because according to God, sin and guilt longer exist!

> When you were dead in your sins and in the uncircumcision of your sinful nature, God made you alive with Christ. **He forgave us all our sins.**
>
> —Colossians 2:13

The opposite of guilt is to be innocent; guiltless, blameless, clean, irreproachable, pure, righteous, virtuous and faultless. **God has forgiven you**. This is who we are in Christ! Therefore, we need to start walking by this truth and NOT by what our feelings and emotions are dictating to us.

No Condemnation!

Condemnation means to judge a person as guilty and liable for punishment. It is the sentence, judgment or the punishment for sin. So when we judge ourselves as bad, guilty, wrong or to blame then we are condemning ourselves. The devil wants you to feel condemned and trapped in the pain of your past. But as we have just discovered, the truth is that Jesus has already paid the price for our sins. So for those who believe in Jesus, there is no longer any punishment for sin. There is no root to these feelings, because as far as God is concerned, our past is gone. Therefore, because our sins no longer exist, condemnation should not even be in our thinking or vocabulary!

> Therefore, there is now **no condemnation** for those who are in Christ Jesus, because through Christ Jesus the law of the Spirit of life set me free from the law of sin and death.
>
> —Romans 8:1–2

> He who believes in Him [who clings to, trusts in, relies on Him] is not judged [he who trusts in Him never comes up for judgment; for him there is no rejection, no **condemnation**—he incurs no damnation]...
>
> —John 3:18, amp

> I assure you, most solemnly I tell you, the person whose ears are open to My words [who listens to My message] and believes and trusts in and clings to and relies on Him who sent Me has (possesses now) eternal life. And **he does not come into judgment** [does not incur sentence of judgment, will not come under **condemnation**], but he has already passed over out of death into life.
>
> —John 5:24, amp

> Christ purchased our freedom [redeeming us] from the curse (doom) of the Law [and its condemnation] by [Himself] becoming a curse for us, for it is written [in the Scriptures], "Cursed is everyone who hangs on a tree (is crucified)."
>
> —Galatians 3:13, amp

When we apply this truth to our lives, we will be free to feel good about ourselves, and free to declare the truth that no matter what we have done, through Jesus **we have already been forgiven and made righteous**, loved, accepted and approved in the eyes of God. Therefore, stop condemning yourself and start focusing on and **declaring the truth of what Jesus has done for you. Death and life are in the power of your tongue** (Proverbs 18:21), so declare the truth of God's Word in this area to experience freedom once and for all from guilt, shame and condemnation.

> He **has delivered** us from the power of darkness and conveyed us into the kingdom of the Son of His love, in whom **we have** redemption through His blood, the **forgiveness of sins**.
>
> —Colossians 1:13–14, NKJV

> So if the Son sets you free, you will be free indeed.
>
> —John 8:36

The next time Satan comes to accuse you of your past, or torments you with feelings of guilt, shame or condemnation, remind yourself of the truth that **you have been** set free and then declare that truth by saying out aloud "NOT GUILTY!"

God sees and counts you worthy because you are the righteousness of God! He doesn't see your faults, your past or shortcomings. He only sees His precious Son in you. And when you gain the revelation of this truth, it will change the way that you see yourself and how you relate to Him. Releasing the fullness of what God has freely provided and already given to you will then be a whole lot easier!

Righteousness Comes Only Through Faith!

Righteousness is the quality of being right or having a right standing with God and this comes only through faith in Jesus.

> "Behold, the days come," saith the Lord, "that I will raise unto David a righteous Branch, and a King shall reign and prosper, and shall execute judgment and justice in the earth. In His days Judah shall be saved, and Israel shall dwell safely: and this is His name whereby he shall be called, THE Lord OUR RIGHTEOUSNESS."
>
> —Jeremiah 23:5–6

Jesus is our righteousness! When we accepted Jesus as our Lord and Saviour, we became the righteousness of God. Our actions or lifestyles cannot make us righteous. Isaiah 64:6 tells us that all our righteous acts are like filthy rags! So being a "good" person or doing "good works" to earn something from God means absolutely nothing.

> Now we know that whatever the law says, **it says to those who are under the law**, that every mouth may be stopped, and all the world may become guilty before God. Therefore **by the deeds of the law no flesh will be justified** in His sight, for by the law is the knowledge of sin.
>
> —Romans 3:19–20, NKJV

> ...**a man is not justified by the works of the law but by faith in Jesus Christ**, even we have believed in Christ Jesus, that we might be justified by faith in Christ and not by the works of the law; for **by the works of the law no flesh shall be justified**.
>
> —Galatians 2:16, NKJV

Justified means to be declared just, made righteous and accepted of God, and this does not come through following the works of the law or through our performance, but only through faith in Jesus. Praise God! We are no longer under the law because as new covenant believers we are now under grace!

> But now the righteousness of God apart from the law is revealed, being witnessed by the Law and the Prophets, even the righteousness of God, through faith in Jesus Christ, **to all and on all who believe**. For there is no difference; for all have sinned and fall short of the glory of God, **being justified freely by His grace** through the redemption that is in Christ Jesus, whom God set forth as **a propitiation by His blood, through faith**, to demonstrate His righteousness, because in His forbearance God had passed over the sins that were previously committed, to demonstrate at the present time His righteousness, that He might be just and **the justifier of the one who has faith in Jesus**.
>
> —Romans 3:21–26, NKJV

We were justified freely by the grace of God through the redemptive work of Jesus! **Propitiation** literally means that Jesus was our atoning sacrifice that appeased God's wrath. Jesus fulfilled and replaced the Old Testament sacrificial system by offering Himself as the final, once-and-for-all sacrifice of atonement through the shedding of His blood (Hebrews 9:11–15, 23–28; 10:10–14). By His one act of righteousness, salvation is now a free gift for all who believe in Him.

> Christ is the end of the law so that there may be **righteousness for everyone who believes**.
>
> —Romans 10:4

> God made Him who had no sin to be sin for us, so that in Him we might become the righteousness of God.
>
> —2 Corinthians 5:21

Through the finished work of the cross, Jesus accomplished several things:

- **He paid the penalty of sin**. Jesus bore our sins (and the sins of the whole world) so that we can receive forgiveness. He became sin so that we can become the righteousness of God. He was the propitiation, the atoning sacrifice and He appeased God's wrath against sin. There is now therefore no condemnation (punishment for sin) for those who are in Christ Jesus.
- **He destroyed the power of sin**. Jesus paid the price for sin! He redeemed us from the curse and condemnation of the law by becoming a curse for us. He redeemed and delivered us so that we can be set free from bondage and slavery to sin.
- **He totally removed the stain of sin** by washing and cleansing us with His blood. We have been cleansed from guilt, shame, condemnation and punishment of sin. It says in 1 Corinthians 6:11 that we were **washed, sanctified**, (made holy, consecrated and set apart) and **justified** (declared just, made righteous and accepted). In 1 John 1:7, Amp, it says that we have been cleansed from sin and guilt **in all its forms and manifestations**! This means we are **not guilty**!
- **He destroyed the veil of separation that sin caused**! We are now reconciled and made right with God. We have a relationship

> with Him because we are justified and sanctified. We will never again be separated from Him. When we believed in Jesus, we were made holy and blameless in His sight. We were accepted, loved and approved, and **sealed with the Holy Spirit**, who is the guarantee of our salvation until Jesus returns for us (Ephesians 1:4, 6, 13).

All we need to do to receive the free gift of righteousness from God is to say **yes** to Jesus! And when we do this, we instantly receive forgiveness of sins, and are delivered and cleansed from the stain of sin and all its power! Our old man (sinful nature) dies and we are born again by the Spirit of God. Through His very Spirit we receive His righteousness, holiness, power and love. From that moment on we have right standing with God and we can experience unbroken fellowship with Him. And this comes, not by following the law or by our performance, but by God's grace through faith in Jesus' atoning sacrifice!

Leave The Past In The Past!

> So if the Son sets you free, you will be free indeed.
>
> —John 8:36

Can you now see that it doesn't matter what we have done in the past? God **has** forgiven ALL sins, past, present, and future! We have been forgiven and God remembers our sins no more! As far as God is concerned, it is ALL gone! So Satan has no right to enforce your past and make you feel guilty, condemned, punished or unworthy to receive from God—**unless you allow him to**!

> I, even I, am He who **blots out and cancels your transgressions**, for My own sake, and **I will not remember your sins**.
>
> —Isaiah 43:25, amp

If God does not consider or remember our sins, then we need to make the decision to not remember them either! We are called to forget the former things and not dwell on the past (Isaiah 43:18). We need to learn how to forget our past because it is no longer of any importance!

> And, beloved, if **our consciences** (our hearts) **do not accuse us** [if they do not make us feel guilty and condemn us], we have confidence (complete assurance and boldness) before God.
>
> —1 John 3:21, AMP

It is also important to realise that not every spiritual attack is of the devil. Sometimes, we can be our own worst enemy and make a mess of things by ourselves. Because God does not condemn us, we need to make sure that we don't allow our own hearts to condemn us either. We need to make the decision to forgive, forget and let go of the past!

Before the apostle Paul knew Christ, he persecuted and killed Christians. If anyone had a reason to feel guilty, it was Paul. But Paul knew how to deal with his past and he led by example. He considered everything he did and who he was before Christ as dung:

> Yea doubtless, and I count all things but loss for the excellency of the knowledge of Christ Jesus my Lord: for whom I have suffered the loss of all things, and **do count them but dung**, that I may win Christ, and be found in Him, not having mine own righteousness, which is of the law, but that which is through the faith of Christ, the righteousness which is of God by faith: that I may know Him, and the power of His resurrection...
>
> —Philippians 3:8–10, KJV

> Brothers, I do not consider myself yet to have taken hold of it. But one thing I do: **Forgetting what is behind** and straining towards what is ahead, I press on towards the goal to win the prize for which God has called me heavenward in Christ Jesus.
>
> —Philippians 3:13–14

Most of us **need to be delivered from ourselves**! We need to lose "self" consciousness or a "sin" consciousness and gain a "God" consciousness. Self-consciousness is self-awareness, where our focus becomes all about "me". We must get over our "self" and begin to believe who we are in

Christ and what **we have received** in Him. From now on, count yourself dead to sin, guilt, shame, condemnation and whatever happened in your past, and start counting yourself alive to God!

> I have been crucified with Christ; it is no longer I who live, but Christ who lives in me; and the life which I now live in the flesh I live by faith in the Son of God, who loved me and gave Himself for me.
>
> —Galatians 2:20, nkjv

Begin to look at yourself through the eyes of faith (by what God's Word says about you). Even though in the natural you may not yet believe it, continue to replace the lies by meditating on and declaring the truth of what God's Word says. When you believe the truth, the devil has no more ammunition! The **very second** you begin to feel challenged, use your authority in Jesus, and resist and replace the lies immediately. Always remember the truth that in Christ "you were washed...you were sanctified...you were justified in the name of the Lord Jesus and by the Spirit of our God" (1 Corinthians 6:11, nkjv).

God's Medicine For Guilt, Shame And Condemnation

If you want to walk in victory over guilt, shame and condemnation once and for all, then it is imperative that you begin to meditate on and declare the truth in God's Word, renewing your mind and transforming the way you see yourself and what you believe about your past.

> Therefore if any person is [ingrafted] in Christ (the Messiah) he is a **new creation** (a new creature altogether); the old [previous moral and spiritual condition] has passed away. Behold, the fresh and new has come!
>
> —2 Corinthians 5:17, amp

If you are in Christ, then you are a **new creation**! Stop living by your feelings, emotions and memories of the past and start living by the truth! Stop looking to your "self", that is, to what you can do, and start looking to what Jesus has done! We need to stop feeding on the lies and start feeding on the truth!

We also need to stop allowing the outer natural man to dominate and instead bring all of our natural thinking, reasoning and understanding into agreement with the indwelling Spirit of truth. We do this by learning to live out of the reality of who we are in Christ and what we have inherited in Him by renewing our minds and acting on this truth.

Another important step is to **stop giving power to your past**! When I say this, I am not talking about denial but rather reminding your mind, flesh and the devil the truth of what Jesus has done. When you do this, you stop your past from controlling your future! Remind yourself of who you are in Christ, where you are seated and what you have inherited as a believer. It is up to us to take what Jesus has done and bring the feelings, emotions and thinking into line with that truth.

Therefore, make a decision to lay your past, no matter what happened, at the foot of the cross. Jesus took your pain, shame, weaknesses and distresses. He suffered—He was beaten, wounded and bruised. He paid the price so that you can be forgiven, cleansed, healed, delivered, and set free from the pain, stain and power of sin in all of its forms and manifestations! The work that Jesus did on the cross has made you whole.

We need to appropriate the finished work of the cross into every area of our lives. In the same way we would resist and oppose physical pain and symptoms of sickness and disease, we need to resist emotional pain, thoughts, memories, feelings and emotions. **Don't submit** to them by focusing or meditating on them. **Instead, resist**, which means oppose, withstand and strive against them! Replace them with the truth of who you are, where you are seated and what belongs to you in Christ. Make the decision to say only what God says about your past. Remember that "confess" means to agree with, (not to refuse or deny,) to declare openly, speak out freely. Therefore, with your mouth say only what God says about you and what He has done for you through His Son!

What God Says...

"...whoever believes on Him will not be put to shame."

—ROMANS 9:33, NKJV

"Do not be afraid; you will not suffer shame. Do not fear disgrace; you will not be humiliated. You will forget the shame of your youth..."

—ISAIAH 54:4

But if we [really] are living and walking in the Light, as He [Himself] is in the Light, we have [true, unbroken] fellowship with one another, and the blood of Jesus Christ His Son cleanses (removes) us from all sin and guilt [keeps us cleansed from sin in all its forms and manifestations].

—1 JOHN 1:7, AMP

"Come now, let us reason together," says the Lord. "Though your sins are like scarlet, they shall be as white as snow; though they are red as crimson, they shall be like wool."

—ISAIAH 1:18

I, even I, am He who blots out and cancels your transgressions, for My own sake, and I will not remember your sins.

—ISAIAH 43:25, AMP

When you were dead in your sins and in the uncircumcision of your sinful nature, God made you alive with Christ. He forgave us all our sins.

—COLOSSIANS 2:13

Therefore, there is now no condemnation for those who are in Christ Jesus, because through Christ Jesus the law of the Spirit of life set me free from the law of sin and death.

—ROMANS 8:1–2

Christ is the end of the law so that there may be righteousness for everyone who believes.

—Romans 10:4

...But you were washed, but you were sanctified, but you were justified in the name of the Lord Jesus and by the Spirit of our God.

—1 Corinthians 6:11, NKJV

What You Can Say...

Let the redeemed of the Lord say so! Begin to make the following scriptural confessions over your life!

For it is by ***free grace*** *(God's unmerited favour) that I am saved (delivered from judgment and made partakers of Christ's salvation) through my faith. And this salvation is not of my own doing, it came not through striving, but it is* ***the gift of God****; not because of works (not the fulfilment of the law's demands), lest I should boast. (It is not the result of what I could possibly do, so I cannot pride myself in it or take glory to myself.)* (Ephesians 2:8, AMP)

Praise be to the God and Father of my Lord Jesus Christ, who has blessed me in the heavenly realms with every spiritual blessing in Christ. For He chose me in Him before the creation of the world ***to be holy and blameless in His sight****. In love He predestined me to be* ***adopted as His child*** *through Jesus Christ, in accordance with His pleasure and will—to the praise of His glorious grace, which He has freely given me in the One He loves. In Him* ***I have redemption through His blood, the forgiveness of sins****, in accordance with the riches of God's* ***grace that He lavished on me*** *with all wisdom and understanding.* (Ephesians 1:3–8)

I praise the Lord, with all my soul, and I forget not all His benefits—He has ***forgiven all my sins*** *and healed all my diseases.* (Psalm 103:2–3)

He ***has delivered*** *me from the power of darkness and conveyed me into His kingdom, and I* ***have*** *redemption through His blood, the* ***forgiveness of sins.*** (Colossians 1:13–14, NKJV)

Because I am in Christ, I am a ***new creation*** *(a new creature altogether). The old (previous moral and spiritual condition) has passed away. Behold, the fresh and new has come!* (2 Corinthians 5:17, AMP)

I count all things but loss for the excellency of the knowledge of Christ Jesus my Lord, and ***do count them but dung,*** *that I may be found in Christ, not having my own righteousness, which is of the law, but that which is through the faith of Christ, the righteousness which is of God by faith, that I may know Him, and the power of His resurrection.* (Philippians 3:8–10, KJV)

I do not consider myself yet to have taken hold of it. But one thing I do: ***Forgetting what is behind*** *and straining towards what is ahead, I press on towards the goal to win the prize for which God has called me heavenward in Christ Jesus.* (Philippians 3:13–14)

I have been crucified with Christ. It is no longer I who live, but Christ lives in me, and the life which I now live in the flesh I live by faith in the Son of God, who loved me and gave Himself for me. (Galatians 2:20, NKJV)

The blood of Jesus has cleansed and removed me from all sin and guilt, in all its forms and manifestations. (1 John 1:7, AMP)

I have my heart sprinkled with Jesus' blood and cleansed from a guilty conscience. (Hebrews 10:22)

I have been forgiven! (Psalm 32:5, Hebrews 8:12, 1 John 1:9)

God has blotted out my sins and remembers my sins no more. So I won't either! (Isaiah 43:25)

Because I am in Christ, I am not condemned. (John 3:17–18, Romans 8:1–2)

I have Jesus' righteousness because of my faith in Him. (Romans 3:22)

God made Him who had no sin to be sin for me, so that in Him I have become the righteousness of God. (2 Corinthians 5:21)

I know the truth and that truth has set me free. (John 8:32)

I will go out in joy and be led forth in peace. (Isaiah 55:12)

Overcoming Doubt And Unbelief

SIXTEEN

"Do not be afraid; **only believe**" (Mark 5:36).

Through our faith in Jesus, we have already received everything we need to rule and reign in life. Once we know what we have inherited through Jesus, we then need to learn how to walk by this truth and not by sight, feelings and symptoms, or by what the natural realm is dictating to us. If we do focus on the natural circumstances instead of the truth found in God's Word, then that is when doubt and unbelief can come in, and if entertained, they will take root, grow and bear fruit in our lives.

Because we live in a fallen world, we will all face doubts from time to time. Experiencing doubt is not wrong in itself, but it is what we do with the doubts that matter. If we continue to feed on our doubts, we can become so overwhelmed that we may see no way out of our situation. So while doubt and unbelief cannot change God's unconditional love towards us, they can change our ability to walk in what God has freely provided for us. This very thing happened to the children of Israel. God had said to Moses, "Send men to spy out the land of Canaan, **which I am giving** to the children of Israel" (Numbers 13:2). Moses was called to lead the children of Israel into the Promised Land. God had given them the entire land and victory over all its inhabitants. When they reached the borders of the land Moses sent 12 spies ahead to check it out. But instead of returning with a positive report and a strategy to take the land, 10 of the 12 spies came back with a negative report (Numbers 13:27–28, 30–33). And because the people didn't mix God's Word with faith, but instead believed the spies' negative report, the Israelites spent 40 years wandering in the wilderness. They missed the promise of God and on possessing their Promised Land due to their doubt and unbelief.

Therefore, it is necessary that we don't fall into the same trap that these Israelites did, but instead learn how to walk in victory over doubt and unbelief so that we can walk unhindered in the fullness of God's provision.

The dictionary defines "doubt" as, a feeling of uncertainty or lack of conviction, to disbelieve a person or their word, or to fear or be afraid of something. *Strong's Concordance* defines "doubt" to mean not convinced or fully persuaded. "Unbelief" in the dictionary is defined as an absence of faith, and *Strong's Concordance* explains "unbelief" as, faithlessness, disbelief, hardness of heart, or destitution of (spiritual) perception! So by these definitions we can clearly see that doubt stops us from believing God's Word, and unbelief is a lack of faith or trust in God, His Word and in His power and ability. Doubt and unbelief place the facts, symptoms or circumstances above the truth of who God is and what He has said in His Word.

Trust And Believe That God Is Good

If we don't believe that we can trust God for our situation, then we need to spend time building and strengthening our relationship with Him by meditating on the truth of who He is as revealed through Jesus. We need to continually remind ourselves that His plans are always to bless and prosper us and that He is a rewarder of those who earnestly seek Him (Jeremiah 29:11, James 1:17, Hebrews 11:6). Once we know this truth, we will be able to lean our entire human personality on God in absolute trust and confidence in His power, wisdom and goodness (Colossians 1:4, AMP; Hebrews 10:22–23, AMP; 2 Timothy 3:15, AMP).

If we don't know that God is only good and that what He has done through His Son is already our inheritance, it will be easy to lose sight of the truth in His Word. But when we know the One who has promised, believing His Word will be simple. Abraham and Sarah knew who God was and this enabled them to be fully persuaded that He would do what He had promised them.

> ...not being weak in faith, he did not consider his own body, already dead (since he was about a hundred years old), and the deadness of Sarah's womb. **He did not waver at the promise of God** through unbelief, but was strengthened in faith, giving glory to God, and **being fully convinced** that what He had promised He was also able to perform.
>
> —Romans 4:19–21, NKJV

> By faith Sarah herself also **received strength to conceive seed**, and she bore a child when she was past the age, **because she judged Him faithful** who had promised.
>
> —Hebrews 11:11, NKJV

Abraham and Sarah received strength (God's miracle working power), which enabled them to conceive in spite of their natural circumstances. I believe that the key to their breakthrough was that they **considered** or **judged God faithful**. When they "considered" God, it meant that they were not considering their natural facts. We know that they weren't in denial because they had faced the natural facts that their bodies were as good as dead. BUT they were fully convinced that God was able to perform what He had promised.

Overcome Natural Thinking

For many who are wanting to see God's Word come to pass in their lives, their greatest obstacle or challenge will not be their diagnosis or natural circumstances, but rather their thinking and understanding. In other words, **how they see their situation.** This is because for most of us our natural thinking and understanding will always default to looking at and focusing on the natural realm. If we place more emphasis on our natural circumstances, then they will become larger and more powerful in our thinking and this causes us to lose sight of the truth in God's Word. Therefore, we need to change how we see our natural situation by overcoming our doubts and fears, and guarding what we believe in our heart so that we can see, think, feel and act according to what the Word says, and not according to the natural circumstances.

God's Kingdom Is A Supernatural Spiritual Kingdom!

To understand what God's kingdom is and how it works, we first need to understand that His kingdom is spiritual, not natural, and that this spiritual kingdom is more real than the natural realm. In fact, the unseen spiritual realm created this seen natural realm!

> By faith we understand that the worlds were framed by the word of God, so that the things **which are seen** were not made of things **which are visible.**
>
> —Hebrews 11:3, NKJV

The unseen created the seen! We are also told that everything in the universe is being upheld, maintained and sustained by God's mighty Word of power (Hebrews 1:3).

The Spiritual Realm CHANGES The Natural Realm

To be in a desperate situation with no hope and all seems lost is distressing. But we need to learn to keep our focus and thinking out of the natural circumstances and limitations of the natural world, and instead learn to release God's power, which can change what's happening in the natural world.

> But the natural man does not receive the things of the Spirit of God, for they are foolishness to him; nor can he know them, because they are **spiritually discerned.**
>
> —1 Corinthians 2:14, NKJV

We are called to live as strangers in this world (1 Peter 1:1; 2:11). Unfortunately, many of God's children are strangers not to this world, but to His kingdom and how it works. Therefore, we need to learn how to be spiritually minded so that we can continue to see God's power released in our lives.

See Beyond The Natural

We interact in this natural realm with our five natural senses. But did you know that we have spiritual senses too? Our natural senses keep us operating in the natural realm while our spiritual senses keep us operating in the spiritual realm of God's kingdom. When we stop looking at our lives through our natural eyes and start looking through the eyes of our spirit (through the eyes of faith, by what God's Word says), then the spiritual realm will become more real to us than the natural realm.

When we first discover the truth of what we have received through the finished work of the cross, our natural circumstances may seem worlds apart from that truth. Everything in the natural can seem to be against us. We can be in debt, be broke, have no education, have a rotten past, be infertile, have an incurable disease, or be constantly sick and hurting. But nothing in the natural can disqualify you from walking in God's provision—unless you allow it to. Continue to meditate on God and His Word until your perspective changes and you see yourself with what He has provided for you. Look past the natural hindrances that are preventing your breakthrough and look only to the solution. See your situation through the eyes of faith (through what the Word says you have through the finished work of the cross) and stop looking at your circumstances with a natural mindset!

When Joshua and Caleb spied out the land, they were able to look past the natural circumstances. They looked through the eyes of God's promise. They saw that the giants in the land could easily be defeated. However, the other 10 spies along with the children of Israel focused on the natural hindrances over God's promise and provision. Their fear of the giants and the natural circumstances caused them to doubt God's supernatural power and ability, and the credibility of His Word. As a result, their perspective changed to the point where, instead of seeing themselves with the victory, they felt and saw themselves like "grasshoppers in our own sight" (Numbers 13:33, NKJV). They were defeated in their own sight because they couldn't see how God was going to get them into the Promised Land past the giants. They looked at all the "mountains of impossibility" they faced in the natural realm, and they forgot the promise of God. We too can fall into the same trap when we look at our own "mountains of impossibility", such as debt, sickness or disease, or our adverse symptoms, diagnosis or circumstances. We need to be like Joshua and Caleb and look at our natural circumstances through the filter of God's Word, so that we are also able to see through the eyes of victory rather than through our natural eyes of defeat!

BELIEVE AND DO NOT DOUBT IN YOUR HEART!

> "Have faith in God", Jesus answered. "I tell you the truth, if anyone says to this mountain, 'Go, throw yourself into the sea,' and **does not doubt in his heart but believes** that what he says will happen, it will be done for him.
>
> —MARK 11:22–23

Did you know that the heart is the place where we decide which report we are going to believe? When the Bible says to believe and not doubt in our hearts, it isn't talking about the physical blood pump but the spiritual centre, substance and essence of who we are, what we think and feel, and the centre of what we believe.

When the truth in God's Word is established in our hearts, then out of our hearts can flow the wellsprings of life (Proverbs 2:20–23). Therefore, we need to spend time meditating on the truth of God's Word until it becomes real and alive to us personally and we believe and do not doubt in our hearts what it says.

Romans 10:17 tells us that faith comes by hearing the message of Christ and this message is found in the Word of God. In the same way that you heard the good news of Jesus and accepted Him as your Saviour, listen to and meditate on His Word so that you will see the fullness of what your salvation contains. Continue until this truth goes from information to revelation.

> If any of you lacks wisdom; he should ask God, who gives generously to all without finding fault, and it will be given to him. But when he asks, **he must believe and not doubt**, because he who doubts is like a wave of the sea, blown and tossed by the wind. That man should not think he will receive anything from the Lord; he is a double-minded man, unstable in all he does.
>
> —JAMES 1:5–8

We need to understand that doubt first enters when we take our focus off God and His Word, or when we are more focused on our natural circumstances. Throughout my ministry, I have seen many believers let go of the truth in God's Word through discouragement or through not seeing any immediate changes to their circumstances. They expected instant results, and while this can and often does happen, generally, the process of information becoming revelation and then seeing the manifestation of that can take time. If we want to see the breakthrough, we need to spend time meditating on the truth in God's Word until the revelation comes. The definition of "meditate"—immersing your whole self in the truth of the Word by picturing, pondering, imagining, studying, and musing it over, while also muttering, uttering and speaking forth this truth to yourself with the words of your mouth—implies a period of time.

Remember also that God's Word is His seed on this earth and this is how His kingdom comes and grows in our lives. By comparing His Word with a seed, we see that there is a process of time between when a seed has been planted and when we see the mature fruit-bearing plant. Meditating on God's Word, therefore, is not meant to be a one-off occurrence but rather a lifestyle of feeding on God's truth and seeing it outwork and bear much fruit!

Go Take The Land!

God had given the Israelites the command to go TAKE THE LAND. He had already given them the land; they just had to go and possess it (Numbers 13:1–2). God had given the responsibility to possess the land to them! It was their land BUT through their eyes of doubt and unbelief they rejected God's Word and promise to them.

If you want to possess what God has freely provided for you through Jesus, then you too need to GO and possess the land! Did you know that the word "possess" means, to seize, to get, or to grasp? This means that you do something! It's an attitude where you are so determined to see the breakthrough that you don't let go of the promise. You keep trusting, believing and pressing through past the natural hindrances until you see the provision manifest in your life. This isn't about self-effort in terms of working or trying to earn your breakthrough, but is simply about having an unwavering attitude that is determined to possess what already belongs to you. Begin to see it, feel it and embrace it. Go possess your Promised Land right now!

What To Do With Doubt And Unbelief

One of the best ways you can overcome doubt and unbelief is by continuing to feed on the truth of what God's Word says regarding your situation. Don't just skim over the surface of the Word. Instead, spend time meditating on it until you believe it. I encourage you also to stay focused on who God is and not on what the natural facts are saying or doing.

Below are some ways to help you in this process:

- **Make the decision** that God's Word is true and act on that in everything you think, say and do.
- **Make the decision** to continue to renew your mind and guard your heart and not let go of the truth of what God has said in His Word.
- **Remind yourself that God is always good** and that He is for you and not against you!
- **Remind yourself of all the attributes and benefits of God**: He has forgiven all your sins and healed all your diseases (Psalm 103:1–3). He has also given you every spiritual blessing in Christ (Ephesians 1:3).
- **Fix your eyes on Jesus**, the author and perfecter of your faith. You do this by focusing on the finished work of the cross and remembering that you already have everything you need to walk in victory. It is finished—you already have the inheritance!
- **Fight the good fight of faith**. This means to fight against doubt, unbelief, natural sight and senses, feelings, emotions, symptoms, your diagnosis and natural circumstances, and to rest in what God says instead.
- **Worship and thank God for who He is**! We don't worship God to move Him, but to move ourselves to a position where we can believe His goodness and trustworthiness and receive what He has provided. When you look beyond the natural doubt and discouragement and press into God for who He is, the discouragement will soon leave and you will be more aware of His presence! His peace and joy will begin to strengthen and

flow from your life. You will also be in a better position to hear His voice and to be led by His Spirit into your victory. We don't praise and worship God to try and get victory, we praise, thank and worship Him because He has already given us the victory!

- **Love others as yourself!** I have personally found that what has helped me in my journey is to pray and support someone else in their journey. Shaun and I encourage those in church, in my online support groups and ministry meetings, to do exactly that. I have found that those who are able to take the focus off themselves and pray for someone else have discovered how to hear God's voice and leading for others, which in turn enables them to eventually hear and be led by the Lord for their own lives. I personally have found that as I have received something to share with someone else, the same "word of encouragement" has blessed and helped me in my own personal journey.

- **Strengthen yourself in the Lord!** One thing that saddens me is when I see believers pull back from their relationship with the Lord. If you are struggling in this area, know that He is not withholding anything that Jesus has already purchased and that He has already established in His Word for you. If you stop fellowshipping with Him, it will only prolong your situation, and the pain and emptiness you are feeling. King David knew how to strengthen and encourage himself in the Lord in tough times (1 Samuel 30:6). He wrote, "I WILL bless the Lord at all times; His praise shall continually be in my mouth" (Psalm 34:1 AMP). David constantly meditated on and reminded himself of who God is. He often said of the Lord, "He is my fortress, my tower of strength, my refuge in times of trouble." The reason David was chosen as king over all of Israel and over all his brothers was that he had a heart after the Lord. I encourage you, therefore, to run to God and spend time with Him, getting to personally know Him for who He is. When you know the truth, you will realise that He is on your side and that He has already given you everything you need to experience your breakthrough.

- **Judge God faithful**. Be like Abraham and Sarah who judged God faithful. Don't **waver** through unbelief, but be strengthened in faith. Give glory to God and **be fully convinced** that what **He has provided and performed** in Jesus **already belongs to you**!

Remember always that nothing is impossible for those who believe, so don't waver in doubt and unbelief, but be strengthened in faith and give glory to God for your victory! Don't let go. Keep trusting and believing, and pressing through past the natural hindrances until you see your breakthrough manifest! Begin to see it, feel it and lay hold of it. Go possess your Promised Land right now!

Replacing Fear With Faith

SEVENTEEN

Isn't it so often true that while we may be hoping for the best, in reality we are actually fearing the worst? While it is not a sign of failure to experience fear as everyone will do so at times, the more attention we give to our fears, the more power they can have over us. And if we don't know how to overcome those fears, they can easily end up controlling our lives. I have had many instances in my life where I have been consumed by fear. In fact, I used to be a slave to fear. It ruled my life. I now live in victory over fear, but it wasn't until I learned to overcome that I realised how much fear I had lived with.

Fear will never be your friend! Fear, when unchallenged, will cause us to lose sight of who we are in Christ and what we have already inherited as a believer. When this occurs, we are deceived into thinking that we are weak and powerless. So while faith enables us to trust in God (His nature, character and power) and act on His Word, fear disables that ability.

Fear will always try to exalt itself in our minds to be greater than the power of God and His Word. If we don't know how to gain victory over fear, especially in challenging circumstances, we may not be able to exercise authority over the situation to see God's power released in our lives. Therefore, we need to learn how to **recognise**, **face** and **replace fear**, because fear left unchallenged will not go away on its own.

> For God did not give us a spirit of timidity (of cowardice, of craven and cringing and fawning fear), **but [He has given us a spirit] of power** and of love and of calm and well-balanced mind and discipline and self-control.
>
> —2 Timothy 1:7, AMP

God has not given us a spirit of timidity or fear! He has given us His **Spirit of power** and authority over all the works and power of the enemy (Luke 10:19). **And this includes fear**! Therefore, know and act on this truth instead of allowing fear to torment you any longer.

> Submit yourselves, then, to God. Resist the devil, and he will flee from you.
>
> —James 4:7

The word "resist" in the scripture above means, to oppose, to strive against and to withstand—not to sit back and be passive. We don't need to fight the devil because he has already been disarmed and defeated, but we do need to oppose his attempts to keep us from attaining victory over our thought life and how we see and react to our natural circumstances.

> Be well balanced (temperate, sober of mind), be vigilant and cautious at all times; for that enemy of yours, the devil, roams around **like a lion** roaring [in fierce hunger], **seeking someone** to seize upon and devour. **Withstand him**; be firm in faith [**against his onset**—rooted, established, strong, immovable, and determined]...
>
> —1 Peter 5:8–9, AMP

Did you notice that the scripture above doesn't say that the devil is a roaring lion, but rather he is *like* a roaring lion? The only power he has is the power we allow him to have and generally this comes through falling for his lies and deceptions. And we know that through the finished work of the cross, Jesus disarmed and deprived the devil of his power, removing his teeth and claws. What else does this scripture say? Verse 9 says "**Withstand him**; be firm in faith [**against his onset**—rooted, established, strong, immovable, and determined]..." We are to resist the lies and deceits of the devil at the onset! This means that the very second we begin to question God's truth or become fearful, we need to react. We must make the conscious decision at the onset not to allow worry to take root, or entertain any thoughts or any impressions of fear. Don't ignore these, but resist and replace them by meditating on God's Word and reminding yourself of the truth of who you are in Christ and what belongs to you as a believer. That way you will not only grow in the truth, but also overcome and walk in victory over fear!

Be Anxious For Nothing

Everyone experiences fear in differing degrees. Some may simply have niggling concerns that don't seem to go away, whereas for others, fear can be a controlling force in their lives. While fear can often manifest as a result of a sudden fright, shock or a traumatic situation, more often than not fear develops when we begin to worry or become anxious. There are many fears and concerns that can arise in our lives. The Bible exhorts us, however, not to worry or be anxious about anything (Philippians 4:6). Worry or anxiety left unchecked will grow like a weed and choke the life from the Word of God, preventing it from growing and bearing fruit in our lives. Instead, we need to resist, (oppose, withstand and strive against) any fears or concerns, and they will flee from us!

Watch Your Vision

As we discovered in Chapter 6, faith has vision because it both sees and knows the end result. Faith enables you to see the things you desire before you receive them. As we know, I'm not talking here about looking through your natural eyes but through the eyes of faith. That means to look through the eyes of God's Word because His Word "paints the picture" of what we want to receive.

It is important to note that fear has vision too! While faith pictures us with the answer, meditating on fear pictures us without it!

<u>Fear Versus Faith</u>

Fear has vision:	**Faith has vision:**
Fear has a language (speaks)	Faith has a language (speaks)
Fear sees you without the answer	Faith sees you with the answer
Fear sees the worst result	Faith sees the desired result
Fear links you to the natural	Faith links you to the supernatural

Learn to recognise when you are looking at your circumstances through the eyes of fear so that you can stop, change focus and walk by faith in what God's Word says! I have a girlfriend whose son was suffering from an undiagnosed medical condition. However, all the test results were leaning towards leukaemia. At first, my girlfriend was overcome by fear. She allowed fear to lead her and as she meditated upon the fears, she began to picture her son without hair due to future treatment, picture herself at his funeral and even visiting his grave! After we chatted and prayed together on the phone, she made the decision to picture her son's condition through the eyes of what God's Word said. She began to see him healed, as a young man graduating from high school and university, on his wedding day and on presenting her with her first grandchild. She also exercised her authority over the physical condition of his body and commanded healing to manifest. Needless to say, the test results came back clear of leukaemia and he recovered from that condition!

Fight The Good Fight Of Faith—Fight Fear With The Word!

When we are challenged with an adverse or opposing situation, fear is usually the first thing to surface. While the experience of fear is not wrong in itself, it is how we respond to fear that matters. It is important to note that to walk by faith doesn't mean there is an absence of fear because there will be times when we need to continue to walk by the truth in spite of fear. But if we continue to entertain or submit to our fears, we can lose sight of the truth of God's Word and fear can easily overwhelm us. When this occurs and we react only to the natural circumstances, we may not experience the breakthrough we need. Therefore, we need to learn how to recognise and overcome fear so that we don't lose sight of the truth or give up hope, but rather continue to act on who we are in Christ and on what we are believing for.

When it comes to facing and overcoming fear, we need to know the POWER of God's love towards us!

> There is no fear in love; but **perfect love casts out fear**, because fear involves torment. But he who fears has not been made perfect in love. [The NIV says...fear has to do with punishment.]
>
> —1 John 4:18, NKJV

> For as many as are led by the Spirit of God, these are sons of God. For **you did not receive the spirit of bondage again to fear**, but you received the Spirit of adoption by whom we cry out, "Abba, Father."
>
> —Romans 8:14–15, NKJV

> For I am persuaded that neither death nor life, nor angels nor principalities nor powers, nor things present nor things to come, nor height nor depth, nor any other created thing, shall be able **to separate us from the love of God** which is in Christ Jesus our Lord.
>
> —Romans 8:38–39, NKJV

To have lasting victory over fear, we need to replace our fears by meditating on the truth of what God's Word says about who we are in

Christ, what we have already received and God's unconditional love for us. If we don't, then fear will deceive us into believing in and giving into the strength of the natural situation. We need to trust what God has already established for us in His Word because when we believe the truth, the devil has no more ammunition. Even God trusts His Word. He has exalted His Word above His name (Psalm 138:2). But don't simply quote scripture—the **power** of God is released when you **believe** His Word, **act** on it by declaring that truth, and exercise His power and authority over the situation!

God's Medicine For Fear

I encourage you to meditate on the following scriptures, which deal with the subject of fear, along with those that describe who you are in Christ. Continue to renew your mind with them and make them personal to you by speaking them out as a confession over your life.

What God Says...

> *...do not fear, for I am with you; do not be dismayed, for I am your God. I will strengthen you and help you; I will uphold you with My righteous right hand.*
>
> —Isaiah 41:10

> *...Be strong and courageous. Do not be terrified; do not be discouraged, for the Lord your God will be with you wherever you go.*
>
> —Joshua 1:9, Deuteronomy 31:6

> *...whoever listens to me will live in safety and be at ease, without fear of harm.*
>
> —Proverbs 1:33

> *There is no fear in love; but* ***perfect love casts out fear****, because fear involves torment. But he who fears has not been made perfect in love.*
>
> —1 John 4:18, nkjv

What You Can Say...

Let the redeemed of the Lord say so! Begin to make the following scriptural confessions over your life!

> *God is my refuge and strength, an ever-present help in trouble. Therefore, I will not fear.* (Psalm 46:1–2)
>
> *I will not be afraid but I will trust in God and what His Word says. What can mortal man do to me?* (Psalm 56:3–4)
>
> *In righteousness I am established. Tyranny will be far from me; I have nothing to fear. Terror will be far removed; it will not come near me.* (Isaiah 54:14)
>
> *God did not give me a spirit of timidity (of cowardice, of craven and cringing and fawning fear),* ***but He has given me a spirit of power*** *and of love, and of calm and well-balanced mind, and discipline and self-control.* (2 Timothy 1:7, AMP)
>
> *By faith Christ dwells in my heart! I am* ***rooted deep in love*** *and* ***founded securely on love,*** *so I* ***have the power*** *and* ***am strong to apprehend*** *and grasp,* ***the experience of that love,*** *what is the breadth and length and height and depth of it.* ***I have really come to know practically, through experience myself,*** *the love of Christ, which far surpasses mere knowledge without experience, and I am filled through all my being unto all the fullness of God. I have the richest measure of the divine presence, and have become wholly filled and flooded with God Himself! Now, because of* ***the action of His power that is at work within me,*** *God is able to carry out His purpose and do superabundantly, far over and above all that I dare ask or think infinitely beyond my highest prayers, desires, thoughts, hopes or dreams.* (Ephesians 3:17–20, AMP)

Declaration Over Fear

Fear, I take authority over you and you ARE TO GO in the name of Jesus!

I refuse to give way to any fear because greater is HE who is WITHIN ME than he who is in the world. I have also not been given a spirit of fear because I HAVE BEEN GIVEN a Spirit of POWER.

I walk in victory over all fear and I will let nothing move me from this position!

Transformation Of The Mind

EIGHTEEN

The mind and thought life is one area where many of us struggle with, whether it's from fear, anxiety, worry, memories of our past or from other torments of the mind. We may also struggle to maintain our trust in God because our natural circumstances may appear larger than our faith, which invariably causes us to end up doubting, worrying or fearing the worst. But the real battle is not a lack of faith, our past or our natural circumstances—*the real battle is in the mind*! But there is good news! As a believer in Jesus Christ, you don't have to be a slave to your thought life any longer, because you can learn how to obtain victory over how you think and feel, and maintain a peaceful mind!

The mind is the seat of our mental thought processes. It is the place of understanding, reasoning, calculating, judging, determining or considering. The mind possesses the ability to understand and reason, and it is where our thoughts, feelings, purposes and desires come from.

Along with all of these things, our mind is also where we judge the things of the Word. If we don't guard our mind and keep God's Word at the forefront, then the seed of God's Word may never get the chance to transform us by springing to life, developing roots and growing from information to revelation, where His Word is real and alive to us personally.

> ...to be carnally minded is death, but to be spiritually minded is life and peace.
>
> —Romans 8:6, NKJV

This scripture is speaking of the importance of being spiritually minded instead of carnally minded. To be carnally minded is to be sensually (the sense realm) or naturally minded and guided. We need to walk by the truth in God's Word to be spiritually minded because as the verse above tells us, the mind controlled by the Spirit has life and peace. If you want to have victory over your thought life, then it is important that you understand how you can actively cooperate with the Spirit of God so that He can help you transform your thinking.

The Mind And Physical Symptoms

As we have already discovered, for many of us, the real battle isn't our natural circumstances, but how we see our situation. While the physical realm and our natural circumstances are real, they can be changed by the power of God's kingdom. But for this change to take place, we need to learn to be kingdom-minded and not natural-minded so that we can experience the victory we need.

When it comes to healing, for example, we need to be careful that we don't allow any condition, symptom or diagnosis to appear greater to us than God's healing power. If we think that what we are facing is greater, we will be unable to believe that God wants us well, and consequently, we will be unable to benefit from the healing that He has already provided.

While we don't deny our natural symptoms, we do have the God-given authority to choose whether we are going to receive what comes upon our body and into our mind (positive or negative). God has given us a free will that enables us to make our own choices. Most of us blame Satan for our condition, but Satan can't legally touch our lives without our permission. The only access he has is the access we allow him to have. Change to our condition or situation, therefore, first begins in our mind through the transformation of our thinking. Then, the natural will follow. However, if we allow our natural circumstances, symptoms or the cares of this world to distract us, then these can grow like weeds and choke the life and power of the Word from flowing in our lives (Mark 4:19). This is why it is important that we don't focus on the natural situation, but remain focused on what God has already done through His Son, through the finished work of the cross.

Being Single-Minded

If we want to see God's indwelling resurrection power released to change our natural circumstances, we must make the decision not to be double-minded or tossed to and fro in our thinking. Instead, we must be single-minded in what we are going to believe. Our mind is the root of where the real battle lies.

> If any of you lacks wisdom, he should ask God, who gives generously to all without finding fault, and it will be given to him. But when he asks, he must believe and not doubt, because he who doubts is like a wave of the sea, blown and tossed by the wind. That man should not think he will receive anything from the Lord; he is a **double-minded man**, unstable in all he does.
>
> —James 1:5–8

To be double-minded simply means to be of two minds! It is where we are torn between the flesh (natural facts) and the truth of the Spirit, which is found in God's Word. Therefore, we need to become single-minded, where our natural mind and thinking is in agreement with the spiritual mind that we have in Christ (the mind of the indwelling Spirit), so that we can draw from His knowledge, wisdom, understanding, revelation, fruit, gifts and power.

Our spirit is identical to Jesus' Spirit. It is perfect, complete, holy, blameless and righteous in every way! The Holy Spirit came and dwelled in us upon our salvation (Ephesians 1:13, 17–18). We became one Spirit with Him (1 Corinthians 6:17; 12:13, Ephesians 2:18; 4:4). Through Him we have been given the fullness of Christ complete with His presence, person and power (Romans 1:16, Colossians 2:8–9). So when we read scriptures such as 1 Corinthians 2:16, which says that "we have the mind of Christ" and 1 John 2:20, KJV, which says that we have an unction from the Holy Spirit and we "know all things", they are not talking about our natural man and understanding, but about the mind of the Holy Spirit who dwells within us.

The mind is the determining factor in what we will believe, follow and act upon—flesh (natural) or Spirit (mind of Christ)! We need to bring our natural mind into agreement with the Spirit. This is what the Bible calls "believing with all of our heart". The Holy Spirit is always in agreement with God, but our natural mind can waver between the truth in God's Word and the natural sense realm. Our physical body (the flesh) will follow the winner between the Spirit and the natural man (natural thinking and understanding).

If your mind is contrary to the Spirit, then you are being double-minded because you are thinking differently to how the Spirit thinks (or to how God thinks). The Word of God gives us a perfect representation of how we are to think. God's Word and the Holy Spirit will always agree (1 John 5:7, NKJV).

The Spirit and Word will always say:

> *I can do all things through Christ who strengthens me* (Philippians 4:13).

By Jesus' stripes I was healed and made whole (Isaiah 53:4-5).

I have been forgiven of all my sins and healed of all my diseases (Psalm 103:1–3)

I am the righteousness of God in Christ (2 Corinthians 5:21).

The indwelling Holy Spirit is always thinking this way but if your mind says, "I feel guilty and unworthy," or "I don't feel healed," and you believe that you are guilty, unworthy or not healed, then you are being double-minded and as James 1:7–8 says, you will not receive anything. But when your soul (mind, will and emotions) comes into agreement (becomes single-minded) with the Spirit of truth that knows all things and agrees perfectly with the Bible, the spirit realm begins to have influence in the soul and it will impact the physical or natural seen realm. This is how we see God's power released in our lives!

Wrong Thinking Leads To Strongholds!

Wrong thinking or an uncontrolled mind doesn't develop overnight, but progresses over time through attitudes, emotions, thought patterns or mindsets that we have meditated upon. And if left unchallenged, these will become strongholds in our lives. A stronghold is a belief or thought pattern of defeat where we see no way out, and which causes us to accept something as unchangeable. Just as a natural stronghold is a fortification that protects and defends what it holds inside, so also a stronghold in the mind protects and defends the beliefs it holds—beliefs that are contrary to the Word of God.

Fear and anxiety or guilt, shame and condemnation are just some examples of what can lead to strongholds forming in our lives. In fact, any thought pattern that prevents us from believing the truth or seeing something as changeable can become a stronghold because we become captive to how we see that situation. Strongholds will consequently alter the way we think and therefore how we behave in certain situations. So it stands to reason that if we never challenge those strongholds, we will remain captive and bound not only in our thinking but also to our natural circumstances.

What About Our Feelings And Emotions?

As we have just discovered, to be carnally minded is to be natural or sense realm minded. Unfortunately, the lack of knowledge of the truth and how to walk in this truth means that this carnal state is where many believers function. They are governed by how they feel and see things either through their physical diagnosis, symptoms or circumstances, or through their natural understanding, feelings and emotions. This then dictates their day, how they respond to life and to the world around them. I believe that this is why many don't see the answers to prayer or see any change to their situation when struggling with sickness, disease, pain or natural circumstances. If we want to see God's power released in our lives, we need to learn how to be led by the Spirit and not our natural feelings and emotions.

I used to believe that our feelings and emotions were separate to our thinking, but in reality, our feelings and emotions are conceived and birthed as a result of our thoughts. Our thoughts trigger our feelings, emotions and responses, and consequently, our decisions and actions.

Our thoughts can therefore affect our whole person! How we think can keep us in bondage because this is not only how we view life, form our opinions and beliefs, but is also how we respond to life's challenges.

However, the good news is that we don't have to be governed by our feelings and emotions any longer because our feelings and emotions are subject to change! When our thinking changes, our opinions and beliefs also change along with our feelings and emotions.

How To Gain Victory Over Your Thought Life

> For though we walk (live) in the flesh, we are not carrying on our

> warfare according to the flesh and using mere human weapons. For the weapons of our warfare are not physical [weapons of flesh and blood], but they are mighty before God for the **overthrow and destruction of strongholds**, [inasmuch as **we**] **refute arguments and theories and reasonings** and every proud and lofty thing that sets itself up against the [true] knowledge of God; and **we lead every thought and purpose away captive** into the obedience of Christ (the Messiah, the Anointed One).
>
> —2 Corinthians 10:3–5, amp

I used to believe that when someone was overcome with their feelings, emotions, fear, depression, or was struggling in their thought life, they had to be healed or delivered from it through the laying on of hands and prayer. However, the scripture above shows us that we don't need to seek someone to pray for us where our mind or emotional and mental health are concerned, because we have the authority over our own lives to guard our thoughts, renew our mind and change the way we think.

> Casting down **imaginations,** and every high thing that exalteth itself against the knowledge of God, and bringing into captivity **every thought** to the obedience of Christ.
>
> —2 Corinthians 10:5, kjv

We obtain victory over our thought life by casting down any imagination, argument, thought, theory, reasoning, feeling, emotion, symptom or diagnosis that doesn't line up with the truth within the Word of God. This means that we are to refuse to entertain any thoughts that are contrary to the Word at the time they come to mind. We are to bring all those thoughts captive to what God says rather than being a captive to them. Don't fight the lies of the enemy by simply trying to think happy or positive thoughts. Freedom comes when we renew our minds with God's thoughts and by refusing to accept any wrong thinking. Remember that Satan's strength and power are in deception and lies, whereas our strength and power are in the truth! So the next time you are tempted or challenged, stop and ask yourself, "What does God's Word say about my situation?" Then exercise your authority over the deceptions and lies and replace them with the truth.

Proverbs 23:7, NKJV, says that as a man "thinks in his heart, so is he". The word "thinks" here in the Hebrew is literally translated as, to act as a gatekeeper! What you "keep" or "guard" in your thoughts (by focusing, paying attention to and meditating upon) is what you can become. Just as a gatekeeper is vigilant in exercising his authority by choosing whom he allows to pass, we need to be just as vigilant about what we allow into our minds to think and focus on. If we pay too much attention to our natural situation, such as our symptoms or diagnosis, or even how we feel, then it can cause us to worry, fear or doubt. The negatives of the situation begin to be amplified and we can lose sight of the power of God and the truth in His Word. Knowing this, why allow the negatives to be magnified?

> Do not conform any longer to the pattern of this world, **but be transformed** by the **renewing of your mind**. Then you will be able to test and approve what God's will is—His good, pleasing and perfect will.
>
> —Romans 12:2

Paul exhorts us in this scripture not to conform to the pattern of this world. The word "conform" literally means to have the same form as another in one's mind or character. Paul is saying here that we must be careful that we don't become "shaped" by the thoughts, ways and patterns of this world, but instead be "transformed" by renewing our mind. The dictionary defines the word "transform" as used in this scripture as meaning, to make a thorough or dramatic change in the form, appearance or character. And the word "renewing" literally means to make new. We need to be careful then that we don't allow how the world thinks, sees and responds to things to determine how we live our lives.

We are called to be set apart and dramatically different from the world in our thinking. His Word shows very clearly who Christ is "in us" and the inheritance we have as God's children so that we can see, think and respond on another level. We must starve the negative thoughts, stop reasoning and analyzing, or focusing on the natural facts, and start feeding on the truth! When you know how to focus on God, not on the negatives, and change the way you see your life, then He will be magnified instead! While it can take time to transform our thinking, and the battle may seem constant at first, it is well worth the effort.

> ...be **constantly renewed in the spirit of your mind** [having a fresh mental and spiritual attitude], and put on the new nature (the regenerate self) created in God's image, [Godlike] in true righteousness and holiness.
>
> —Ephesians 4:23–24, amp

We cannot use our natural mind to see spiritual truth or reality! The spiritual world is real but we cannot reach it through using our five natural senses (through the natural man) because spiritual truth is spiritually discerned. If we want to see God's power released, then it is important to note that we change from the inside out—not from the outside in! Many try to change the external, their habits, diet, exercise, hair or clothes, but we need to have a makeover on the inside! When your thinking is transformed, you will no longer be moved by what you "feel" or see, either physically or through your mind's eye. This is what will bring lasting change and victory!

A Renewed Mind Is A Victorious Mind

We can lead a victorious thought life and overcome any evil suggestion. Nowhere in the Bible has God declared that we would not be tempted. Even Jesus was tempted. So when we are tempted with old thought patterns, we can refuse to allow ourselves to dwell on them, or on any evil thing for that matter. The Bible speaks very clearly about the thoughts that we need to possess:

> ...brethren, whatever is true, whatever is worthy of reverence and is honourable and seemly, whatever is just, whatever is pure, whatever is lovely and lovable, whatever is kind and winsome and gracious, if there is any virtue and excellence, if there is anything worthy of

> praise, think on and weigh and take account of these things [fix your minds on them].
>
> —Philippians 4:8, AMP

Think only of things that are going to build you up—not tear you down! If thoughts come in that are not of God then don't allow yourself to dwell on them.

> Cast your burden on the Lord [releasing the weight of it] and He will sustain you; He will never allow the [consistently] righteous to be moved (made to slip, fall, or fail).
>
> —Psalm 55:22, AMP

Remember that God is not going to renew our minds for us. We are totally responsible for what we allow ourselves to think upon. It is in our power to renew our minds. God has given us discipline and self-control and a free will so that we can choose what we are going to do or think.

> ...be clear minded and self-controlled so that you can pray.
>
> 1 Peter 4:7

In this scripture, clear-minded in the Greek means, to be of sound mind (in one's right mind), to exercise self-control, think of one's self soberly, to curb one's passions, desires and impulses, to be temperate. Similarly self-controlled means, to be calm and collected in spirit, to be temperate, dispassionate, circumspect, to be sober-minded, clear-headed, and restrained. We need to learn how to be wise stewards of our bodies (as the temple of the Holy Spirit) and understand that God has given us a free will. We are to not only honor God with what we do in our outer physical body but also within the inner man, with the way we think and feel.

I know firsthand what it is like to be subject to feelings and emotions and to be a slave to your thought life. I lived a life that was constantly harassed by thoughts of condemnation from my past and other evil suggestions. But when I discovered through God's Word that I had the authority to cast down these thoughts, order soon came to my mind and

I have maintained that victory ever since. My mind became renewed to the truth about who I am in Christ and what the Word says about me and about my situation. I was also able to overcome other areas in my life that had been a struggle. For the first time in my life, I experienced peace in my mind rather than being constantly bombarded by a barrage of different thoughts and overwhelmed by my emotions.

I learnt how to be still and to discern and hear God's voice. This enabled me to be led by Him in many other areas of my life. I have since been able to minister to many who have had similar struggles. The majority of those I have ministered to found these problems were exacerbated when they were in a vulnerable position. Many learnt to exercise authority over their thought life and they too are now experiencing lasting victory, not only in this area but in many other areas of their lives as well.

So it is important that we learn to recognise when we are vulnerable and at these times be on guard. There are many concerns in life that can cause us to worry or fear. Therefore, I encourage you not to entertain these thoughts at all. Instead, meditate on and renew your mind with the truth in God's Word until it comes alive and is real to you personally. There is power and life in the Word and as Jesus said, "...you will **know** the truth, and the truth will set you free" (John 8:32, 36).

When your mind has been renewed with God's truth, it will transform your perspective and how you see yourself or your natural situation. You will see yourself as the victor not the victim. You will see yourself with the answer rather than without it. The supernatural will become more real than the natural, and the fullness of God's indwelling kingdom and Word, when acted upon, will begin to outwork in your life!

God's Medicine For A Renewed Mind

I encourage you to meditate on the following scriptures, which deal with the mind and thought life. Make them personal to you by speaking them out as a confession over your life.

What God Says...

> ...to be carnally minded is death, but to be spiritually minded is life and peace.
>
> —Romans 8:6, NKJV

"Carnal" means the physical realm or the sense realm. We need to walk by the truth in God's Word instead!

> ...as he thinks in his heart, so is he...
>
> —Proverbs 23:7, NKJV

> ...be clear minded and self-controlled so that you can pray.
>
> —1 Peter 4:7

> For though we walk (live) in the flesh, we are not carrying on our warfare according to the flesh and using mere human weapons. For the weapons of our warfare are not physical [weapons of flesh and blood], but they are mighty before God for the **overthrow and destruction of strongholds**, [inasmuch as **we**] **refute arguments and theories and reasonings** and every proud and lofty thing that sets itself up against the [true] knowledge of God; and **we lead every thought and purpose away captive** into the obedience of Christ (the Messiah, the Anointed One).
>
> —2 Corinthians 10:3–5, AMP

> Do not conform any longer to the pattern of this world, **but be transformed** by the **renewing of your mind**. Then you will be able to test and approve what God's will is—His good, pleasing and perfect will.
>
> —Romans 12:2

What You Can Say...

Let the redeemed of the Lord say so! Begin to make the following scriptural confessions over your life!

I have the mind of Christ. (1 Corinthians 2:16)

I choose to only think on those things that are true, worthy of reverence and what is honourable and seemly, just, pure, lovely and lovable, kind and winsome and gracious. (Philippians 4:8, AMP)

I choose to fix my eyes and mind only on Jesus and on what He has already done for me because He is the author and perfecter of my faith. (Hebrews 12:2)

I cast my burdens and cares onto the Lord (releasing the weight of them), and He will sustain me. He will never allow me to be moved (made to slip, fall or fail). (Psalm 55:22, AMP)

For though I walk in the flesh, I am not carrying on my warfare according to the flesh and using mere human weapons. For the weapons of warfare are not physical weapons of flesh and blood, but they are mighty before God for the ***overthrow and destruction of strongholds****. Inasmuch I* ***refute arguments*** *and* ***theories*** *and* ***reasonings*** *and every proud and lofty thing that sets itself up against the true knowledge of God in my mind, and* ***I lead every thought and purpose away captive*** *into the obedience of Christ who is the living Word of God.* (2 Corinthians 10:3–5, AMP)

By Jesus' stripes my mind is healed and whole, every chemical, synapse and hormone works perfectly sending all the right messages to my body. (Isaiah 53:4–5)

I choose to be anxious for nothing, and I draw from God's supernatural peace that surpasses all my understanding and guards my heart and my mind. (Philippians 4:6)

I do not conform any longer to the pattern of this world, but ***I am transformed*** *by the* ***renewing of my mind****. I choose to focus only on the truth of what God's Word says, which is His good, pleasing and perfect will.* (Romans 12:2)

Declaration Over My Sound Mind

Mind, I take authority over you and declare that you are to be sound in the name of Jesus.

I command every part of my brain and mind to be healed and made whole. Every chemical, hormone and synapse is to get into perfect working order!

I refuse to be tormented in my mind because greater is HE who is WITHIN ME than he who is in the world. I have not been given a mind of bondage but one of life and peace.

I cast down every negative thought and everything that does not line up with the truth of who I am in Christ and what I have inherited as a believer!

I cast all my cares, concerns, anxieties and fears upon the Lord.

I HAVE BEEN GIVEN the mind of Christ.

So mind, you are to get in perfect order! You are no longer going to dictate to me what I am going to think upon. I now dictate to you because I have a peaceful mind that only thinks of things that are good, perfect, true, honourable and lovely!

I therefore declare that I walk in victory over all the battles of my mind and I will let nothing move me from this position!

Putting It All Together

How To Walk In Victory When Challenged

NINETEEN

Life is meant to be a great experience, full of the joy and the blessings of the Lord. However, there can be many complications in life that can rob us of these blessings. I see so many needlessly accepting complications in life, such as sickness, disease, pain, poverty, depression, fear, worry and anxiety, all of which manifest as a result of living in a fallen world, simply because they assume it's all part of life. But this couldn't be further from the truth! As we have been discovering throughout this book, the complete work that Jesus did on the cross set us free from **all** forms of sickness, pain, disease, poverty, lack, fear and anxiety no matter what shape or form they manifest in.

I have ministered to many people who have felt that it was easier to cope with their natural circumstances or endure symptoms of pain, sickness or disease because they felt it would require too much energy to exert their authority, especially those who were feeling too unwell, broke, hurt or depressed to do anything. However, James 2:17, Amp, says that faith without works (actions to back up what you believe) is inoperative and powerless. If you want to see a change in your situation, you need to exercise your authority over the circumstances so that you can walk in the provision that is already yours through Christ. Remember always that in Jesus Christ you are more than a conqueror (Romans 8:37) and that you can do all things in Him when you draw from His strength (Philippians 4:13).

When you first begin to walk by the truth in God's Word for your life, and exercise your authority over the situation, it may seem a constant battle at first. Nevertheless, if you continue to persevere and do what the Word says in spite of what is happening in the sense realm, you will soon experience victory.

You will need to know how to walk by faith (in the finished work of the cross) and exercise your authority in the areas you want to overcome. It is more beneficial to do this as a lifestyle and not just when you are challenged with an adverse symptom or situation. This is because when you know what you are doing, you are in a better position if a challenge comes. However, if we only begin to walk by faith when a challenge comes, it is easier to lose focus and feel vulnerable. This doesn't change your position in Christ or what you have already inherited as a believer, but it can affect your ability to see and apply this truth when challenged or when you are faced with an adverse situation.

Walk By Faith, Not By Sight!

I believe that it is important to spend time meditating on the truth of God's Word to help you in your journey. This is not to try to get the victory but to remind yourself that through Jesus you already have the victory. I recommend you continue to meditate on His Word until you come to know it, beyond any doubt, for yourself. I can't stress enough the importance of seeking the Lord for a personal revelation, because it is not sufficient just to know what God's Word says; we need to believe and apply it to our daily lives.

I encourage you to make the decision to be determined to not let go of the truth in the Word and give up or lose hope. Don't look to the natural but instead focus on the solution by meditating on and applying the Word so that you can overcome the natural and experience victory.

I have noticed that when believers have been prepared by meditating on the truth of God's Word, they find it easier to walk by faith (not by sight or appearances). Then, if they are challenged in any way, it is easier to overcome the fear so that they can remain focused on His truth and not on what the natural is doing. This is not to say that you can't obtain the victory if you are challenged, but generally it can be harder to exercise authority over the natural sight or appearances during times of urgency.

We are called to live and walk by faith, not by sight or appearances. Walking by faith by applying God's Word is meant to be a lifestyle and not something you use for a one-time event or for an emergency situation. If you know how to walk by faith, it will be easier to act on what you believe and exercise authority over the situation when you are faced with a complication. You will be able to continue to fight the good fight of faith to overcome and experience the breakthrough. And how do we fight the good fight of faith? By labouring to rest in the finished work of the cross! This may require us to be vigilant against fear and doubt and to exercise authority over the natural circumstances. Generally speaking, we can only act on what we believe to be true or more powerful. So if we haven't spent the time renewing our mind and meditating on the truth of God's Word, then the natural circumstances can very easily overwhelm us.

Remember The Three Simple Keys

If you want to see God's power released to transform your life, remember the three simple keys:

Knowledge or **Information**—knowing what is available, what Jesus has done and your authority in this world.

Faith or **Revelation**—believe you have received what Jesus did through the finished work of the cross by meditating on God's Word until what it says is more real and powerful than what your natural circumstances are dictating. Remember that information needs to become revelation so that God's Word is real and alive to you personally.

Action or **Application**—which simply means to apply the truth to your life, by acting on what you believe and exercising authority over the natural circumstances.

Remember that when it comes to experiencing what Jesus purchased on the cross, it's not about praying or asking God to do what He has already done. Prayer is more about fellowship with God and spending time learning how to be led by His Spirit. The Holy Spirit will warn you of things to come, guide you into all truth and lead you into victory. Make it a priority then to spend time getting to know Him personally, transforming the way you think and the way you see things by continuing to meditate on God's Word until you believe what it says, and you see it as being your final authority. Then, simply act on that truth and the rest will be history.

A Simple Guide To Victory

TWENTY

What can you do when you are threatened with symptoms of sickness, disease, depression, fear, doubt, anxiety, lack or pain?

As we have already discovered, when adverse symptoms or natural circumstances present themselves, we need to command them to change because they will not change when left alone! It is up to us to exercise our God-given authority, especially when it comes to our own lives.

In the event of an emergency, it is important that you have already learnt how to walk by faith (by what you have received through the finished work of the cross) and not by sight or natural appearances. This is important because if you are challenged with an adverse situation or symptom, it is easier to remain focused and not lose sight of the truth in God's Word.

Over the following few pages, I have listed some things that I believe will remind you of who you are in Christ and what you have already inherited so that you don't lose sight of the victory when you are challenged. Once again, it is important that you don't view these points as a formula to follow to attain your desired result. Following a formula or steps without revelation is not only powerless but also leads to frustration. As we have already discovered, we have already received the victory we need upon salvation. We simply need to remind ourselves of this truth and not lose hope or become overwhelmed with the natural circumstances.

Remember the finished work of the cross! Jesus has already paid the price in full for all sin, sickness, disease, pain, shame, rejection, depression, poverty and lack so that you can be forgiven, healed, delivered, prospered and made fruitful in every area of your life! It is finished—the price has been paid and the victory won for you! Therefore, enjoy and declare your victory and all that Jesus has freely provided for you.

Labour to stay in rest! When we look to the natural circumstances, it is easy to lose sight of the truth and become overwhelmed. During times like this, we need to continue to labour to remain in a place of rest, knowing that the work has been done, and we have everything we need to walk in victory. If we lose sight of this truth, we may get caught up in works and striving (doing, trying, struggling) to get the breakthrough. Instead, we need to walk by faith (by what we believe we have received through the finished work of the cross) and not by sight—by the natural realm and senses.

Don't be ruled by fear. Overcome fear with the Word of God and declare what He says concerning your situation. Remember, you have not been given a spirit of fear but one of power, a sound mind and self-control (2 Timothy 1:7). Remember also not to go by your feelings. I know from experience that sometimes it feels too hard when you are challenged or are faced with an emergency. However, regardless of how you feel, remember that you are more than a conqueror (Romans 8:37), and greater is Jesus who is in you than our enemy who is in the world (1 John 4:4). In Christ, you can obtain strength for all things (Philippians 4:13). Also, know that you don't have to wait for the natural course of events to take place. Don't sit back, be passive and assume that everything will be perfect, but be active and continue to walk by faith and declare God's truth over your life!

Meditate and keep focused on the truth. It is easy to lose sight of the power of God and be overwhelmed by the natural circumstances. However, continue to meditate on the truth of what God's Word says. Proverbs 4:20–23 tells us that when God's Word finds place in our heart, it brings healing and health to our flesh and life to our outward circumstances. It's important that you don't base your confidence in what you see (or don't see) in the natural realm. When God's Word becomes your final authority, it doesn't matter what is happening in the natural because you can see His power change and transform the situation!

Remember your authority. As believers in Jesus, we have His authority, power and person living on the inside of us! We are not trying to get power and authority—we already have power and authority because of our position in Christ. We are seated with Christ in heavenly places, far above all rule and authority, power and dominion, and every title that can be given, not only in the present age but also in the one to come (Ephesians 1:21; 2:6).

You HAVE the authority to bind and loose sickness, disease, pain, fear, doubt, depression, anxiety, poverty and lack from your life. If you tell it to be removed, it will be removed. If you tell it to die at the root, it will die at the root. If you resist it, then it must flee! Take authority over your circumstances, symptoms or diagnosis and command any sickness in your body to leave! Command your natural circumstances to change!

Remember the power of your words. We exercise authority over any situation by our words and what we say! God released His power by His Words. If you want to see the power of God released in your life, you need to act on what you believe and use your words too. It is important to note that we don't confess or declare God's Word to make something happen.

We confess (agree with or say the same as) what God says because of **what has already happened**! Confess **what Jesus has done** through the finished work of the cross! Take authority and declare out aloud what God's Word says to that area of your life.

Be anxious for nothing! Peace comes when we are anxious for nothing and can put our trust in God. "And the peace of God, which transcends all understanding, **will guard** your **hearts and your minds** in Christ Jesus" (Philippians 4:7).

Praise and worship. Worship doesn't change God but it sure changes you! Put on some praise and worship music and lift up your heart and voice to God. Offer Him the fruit of your lips as a sacrifice of praise. Psalm 22:3, KJV, tells us that God inhabits the praises of His people and Psalm 9:1–3 says that when God comes, our enemies fall back and perish at His presence. You will need to get your focus off the natural situation and keep it fixed on God. Worship will help you to enter into the awareness of His presence where His life and healing power can flow through you.

Thank God. Give God the glory and thank Him for the finished work of the cross and for what already belongs to you regarding your health, wholeness and safety.

Remember God's strength. There is no beginning or end to God's power because His power has no boundaries. We simply need to learn to use His strength and not do everything on our own because if we do we will quickly tire.

Ephesians 6:10, AMP. In conclusion, be strong in the Lord [**be empowered through your union** with Him]; draw your strength from Him [that strength which His boundless might provides].

Philippians 4:13, AMP. **I have strength for all things** in Christ **who empowers me** [I am ready for anything and equal to anything through

Him **who infuses inner strength into me**; I am self-sufficient in Christ's sufficiency].

Isaiah 40:29, 31. He gives strength to the weary and increases the power of the weak…but those who hope in the Lord will renew their strength. They will soar on wings like eagles; they will run and not grow weary, they will walk and not be faint.

Remember that God is good and He loves you. And finally, regardless of what you go through, God's love is always there for you.

Hebrews 13:5, AMP. …for He [God] Himself has said, I will not in any way fail you nor give you up nor leave you without support. [I will] not, [I will] not, [I will] not in any degree leave you helpless nor forsake nor let [you] down (relax My hold on you)! [Assuredly not!]

Appendices

How To Receive Your Salvation

"For God so loved the world that He gave His one and only Son, that whoever believes in Him shall not perish but have eternal life" (John 3:16).

God loves you so much that He sent His Son Jesus to come and take away the sin of the world (including yours) so that you can receive forgiveness, have a relationship with Him and experience eternal life. Without receiving Jesus, we can't experience that relationship with God.

> ...all have sinned and fall short of the glory of God.
>
> —Romans 3:23

Sin separates us from God and separation from God will lead to death.

> For the wages of sin is death, but the gift of God is eternal life in Christ Jesus our Lord.
>
> —Romans 6:23

Since sin is the problem that separates us from a relationship with God, we need to get rid of it. Simply making the decision to start doing the right thing does not achieve this. God sent His Son to die in our place.

He put on a human form and as Jesus He became "God in the flesh". Because Jesus was sinless, He suffered on the cross in our place by becoming sin so that we can have a right standing with God and be reconciled to Him.

The very moment that you accept Jesus as your Lord and Saviour, you receive an inheritance from God and eternal life. You also receive the forgiveness of all your sins.

> If we confess our sins, He is faithful and just and will forgive us our sins and purify us from all unrighteousness. If we claim we have not

> sinned, we make Him out to be a liar and His word has no place in our lives.
>
> —1 JOHN 1:9–10

We can only have a right standing with God through the atoning death of Jesus Christ on the cross. When **anyone** believes in and receives Jesus' sacrifice, God declares them cleansed from all unrighteousness and in that moment they experience peace with God.

> Therefore being justified by faith, we have peace with God through our Lord Jesus Christ.
>
> —ROMANS 5:1, KJV

When you become a Christian, you are no longer just born of your mother here on this natural earth, but you are now also born into the kingdom of God! You become a child of God.

> ...as many as received Him, to them gave He power to become the sons of God, even to them that believe on His name.
>
> —JOHN 1:12

You receive so much more as well! You will have acceptance, love, joy, peace, patience, kindness, goodness, faithfulness, peace, joy, fruitfulness and self-control. The restoration of your soul is deep, satisfying and lasting! The joy of the Lord will become your strength!

DOESN'T BEING A GOOD PERSON MAKE ME A CHRISTIAN?

Being a Christian is not about good works or about being a good person. You cannot work or earn your ticket to heaven!

> For it is by grace you have been saved, through faith—and this not from yourselves, it is the gift of God—not by works, so that no one can boast.
>
> —EPHESIANS 2:8–9

Going to church, reading the Bible, praying and being a giver are all "things" a Christian does, but they are not what earns his or her salvation. The **only** way into eternal life is through Jesus. Christianity, therefore, is not about going to church and doing the outward things, but about a personal relationship with God our heavenly Father!

> Jesus answered, "**I am the way and the truth and the life. No one comes to the Father except through Me**. If you really knew Me, you would know My Father as well. From now on, you do know Him and have seen Him."
>
> —JOHN 14:6–7

Salvation is not about what you can do for God, but about what **God has done for you**! Therefore, it does not matter who we are, what we have been or what we have done in our past, because our eternal destiny lies with one truth and that is whether we have (or have not) received Jesus!

SO WHAT WILL YOU DO WITH JESUS?

If you have never received Jesus, then you now have a decision to make. God has given you a free will to make your own decision. But if you choose to refuse to receive Jesus free gift, there is nothing else you can do that will make you right with God.

HOW TO RECEIVE JESUS!

> Everyone who calls on the name of the Lord will be saved.
>
> —ROMANS 10:13

Do you want to accept God's provision of His gift of eternal life right now? If so, this is simply done from the moment you say, "**Yes**" to Jesus Christ.

> That if you confess with your mouth, "**Jesus is Lord**," and believe in your heart that God raised Him from the dead, **you will be saved**.

For it is with your heart that you believe and are justified, and it is with your mouth that you confess and are saved.

—ROMANS 10:9–10

If you are ready to say "**Yes**", then say this prayer out loud right now...

SALVATION PRAYER

Father, I thank You for sending Your Son Jesus Christ to die on the cross for me.

I turn away from my old life and I ask You to forgive me for going my own way.

I receive You, Jesus, as my personal Saviour and I choose to follow You and make You Lord of my life.

I ask You to minister to my heart and fill me with Your strength, joy, peace and to fill me with Your Holy Spirit.

I also ask You to guide and help me on how to follow You.

I receive Your perfect will for my life and everything that You died to purchase for me!

AMEN!

Welcome to the family of God!

Your life will never be the same again!

About The Author

Nerida Walker is the mother of four miracle children: Kaitlin, Aidan, and twins, Aaron and Jesse. In 1994, Nerida's husband, Shaun, was diagnosed as sterile, but through the truth in God's Word she conceived and had four children within four and a half years. Based on her own experience, and with a passion to help others struggling through infertility, Nerida founded New Life Ministries—Bringing Life To Barrenness. New Life Ministries is a non-denominational Christian ministry catering to couples who need prayer, encouragement and the knowledge of God's will in any area of childbearing.

Following the conception of her first miracle baby, Nerida wrote *God's Plan For Pregnancy*, a book detailing the truth in God's Word regarding all areas of childbearing. It was written for couples needing truth and encouragement in the areas of infertility, miscarriage, pregnancy, birth and postnatal issues. The book is accompanied by *God's Plan For Pregnancy—Pocket Companion*, a practical guide to help you mix God's Word with faith and to act on what you believe, so that you can see the power of God released in your life to change your natural circumstances.

Since the first edition of *God's Plan For Pregnancy* in 1998, among the thousands of letters and testimonies received were many from husbands, single friends and grandparents. While they weren't necessarily in need of miracles in the areas of fertility and pregnancy, they were blessed by the chapters and godly principles shared in the "Foundations" section of these books, Nerida's way of communicating the truth in God's Word, and the simplicity of how to apply it to their lives. With this in mind, and with a passion to see every believer cross the line from barrenness to fruitfulness in EVERY area of life, Nerida wrote *It Is Finished*, a book revealing how to see God's power released to heal and transform every area of life through the finished work of the cross.

Nerida has also co-written a course on the scriptural principles of healing and lectured for more than five years at a Healing School in Sydney, Australia. Since moving from Sydney to the NSW Central Coast, Nerida has become the director of the Woy Woy Healing Rooms, and alongside her husband, Shaun, is senior pastor of RIVER Christian Church Kariong.

Since 1995, Nerida has ministered to people around the world through the New Life Ministries website, online support group (Women in Faith), her books, and ministry by email. She has seen many healings and many babies conceived and born into the world, at times against incredible odds. Nerida also ministers internationally and at conferences by invitation, most recently in London and Singapore.

In Nerida's heart is a passion to see believers living in the *fullness* of their salvation in every area of life, and to cross the line from barrenness and miscarriage to fruitfulness, from sickness and disease to health, and from lack to the abundance of all that God has provided. Nerida has seen many come to know Jesus, and many believers fall in love with Him all over again, being healed and transformed by the power of God in every area of their lives.

Resource Information

New Life Ministries has a range of audio recordings, DVDs and books available to help you walk by faith in your personal journey. These resources are specifically designed to establish you in the truth of God's Word on healing and contain detailed information on how to apply it to your life.

We have received many letters and emails from all around the world about how our resources have blessed the lives of those who have received them. Many have experienced their breakthrough! We encourage you to share these products as an outreach to others.

Details on where to order our resources are on the New Life Ministries website (www.newlifeministries.com.au). Below is a list of just some of our resources. All new releases will be added to our website as they become available.

Please feel free to write or email to let us know how these resources have personally ministered to you. We look forward to hearing from you!

Audio Messages

Listed below are just some of the audio messages we have available. For a full list and description, visit our online store at www.neridawalker.com

- *The Lord Our Healer*
- *It Is Finished!*
- *Know Your Dominion, Power And Authority And How To Use It*
- *How To See God's Word Come To Pass In Your Life*
- *How To Overcome Depression*
- *How To Overcome Your Past*
- *Transformation Of The Mind*
- *How To Receive Revelation Knowledge*

Fertility Related Resources

Audio Messages

God's Plan For Pregnancy
4-Disc Audio Set
God's Plan For Pregnancy, Created For Fruitfulness, Positively Pregnant and *Childbirth Without Fear.*

Audio messages also sold separately:

- *God's Plan for Pregnancy*
  - *Created For Fruitfulness*
  - *Positively Pregnant*
  - *Childbirth Without Fear*
- *Hannah's Victory*
- *God Is Into Increase Not Decrease!*
- *Stepping Out In Faith*
- *How To See God's Word Come To Pass In Your Life*
- *Victory Over Loss—Testimony By Gillian Robson*
- *Overcoming Infertility—Testimony By Leanne Brooke*

DVD Messages

God's Plan For Pregnancy
2-Disc DVD Set
Nerida shares the truth about God's plan, purpose and will for your conception, pregnancy and childbirth. You will discover how through the finished work of the cross you can lay hold of everything you need to overcome any sickness or disease that causes infertility, miscarriage, pregnancy health issues and complications with the growth and development of your baby, so that you can now go forth and multiply!

Please feel free to write or email to let us know how these resources have personally ministered to you. We look forward to hearing from you!

Books By The Same Author

God's Plan For Pregnancy

Discover God's plan for conception, pregnancy, childbirth and beyond, and how to apply it to your life. This fully comprehensive book is designed to help you overcome fear and walk by faith for all areas of childbearing. It also teaches you how to pray effectively, and contains testimonies from couples who through God's Word overcame incredible odds and received their children!

God's Plan For Pregnancy—Pocket Companion

A companion to *God's Plan For Pregnancy*, which has been specifically designed for you to pop into your handbag so that you can have relevant scriptures and teachings at your fingertips. The *Pocket Companion* is a practical guide to help you mix God's Word with faith and to act on what you believe, so that you can see the power of God released in your life to change your natural circumstances.

Visit www.godsplanforpregnancy.com for more information.

About New Life Ministries

New Life Ministries—Bringing Life To Barrenness is a non-denominational Christian ministry supporting anyone who needs *prayer*, *encouragement* and the *knowledge* of *God's will in any area of childbearing*. This means that if you need support with overcoming infertility, pregnancy health issues, miscarriage, childbirth complications or in the postnatal period, then we are here to help you!

We aim to reach those who are struggling to conceive and/or carry a baby safely to full term, as well as those who are not experiencing complications, but want to gain knowledge of God's Word (His will) for these areas, and practical information on how to apply it to their lives.

We have a passion to teach God's truth in these areas. We desire to see everyone receive revelation on who God is and what He has provided for them, and to see them lay hold of the fullness of the cross and receive their breakthroughs.

If you have in any way been blessed by this ministry, and believe in what we're doing, then we invite you to be a part of it by becoming a New Life Partner.

You can become a New Life Partner through a regular monthly contribution or you can make a one-off donation at any time. Visit our website and complete the Partnership form (found on the New Life Partner's page). Alternatively, you can email us or write to our postal address.

New Life Ministries—Bringing Life To Barrenness

PO Box 593 Forestville NSW 2087 Sydney, Australia
Email: contact@newlifeministries.com.au
Web: www.newlifeministries.com.au